# ultimate

## weird but true

This man looks like he's about to fall into a crevasse. But he's actually standing on a 3-D chalk painting that artist Edgar Mueller drew on the sidewalk.

NATIONAL GEOGRAPHIC
**KIDS**™

# ultimate

## weird but true

NATIONAL
GEOGRAPHIC

WASHINGTON, D.C.

# contents

Tillman's ritual **before** he **rides** is to **chew** on each **tire.**

Tillman the skateboarding dog can travel 328 feet (100 m) in 19.68 seconds. Check out more awesome animals in action on pages 20 and 21.

# CHAPTER 1

# GOING to EXTREMES

## Sky Surfing
<<<

**SPECIAL GEAR:**
skyboard and parachute

**WHY IT'S WEIRD:**
Surfing on air and doing 360s, cartwheels, half twists, and flips while **falling** from **13,000 feet** (3,962 m) in the **air** make this sport a combination of skateboarding, snowboarding, and skydiving.

# ExTREME-LY
## Odd Sports

## Parkour

**SPECIAL GEAR:**
none, just a lot of guts

**WHY IT'S WEIRD:**
Using cities as their playgrounds, athletes do **flips** off buildings, scale walls, and leap across **rooftops** in a single bound.

## Wingsuit Flying

**SPECIAL GEAR:**
wingsuit and parachute

**WHY IT'S WEIRD:**
Skydivers wear special **jumpsuits** with built-in "wings," allowing them to **glide** at 100 miles an hour (160 kph) before releasing a parachute.

# Extreme Ironing

‹‹‹

**SPECIAL GEAR:**
iron, ironing board, and wrinkled clothes

**WHY IT'S WEIRD:**
**Thrill seekers** iron their **laundry** while climbing snowy mountain peaks, scuba diving, water-skiing, bungee jumping, or performing almost any extreme sport.

# Skyaking

›››

**SPECIAL GEAR:**
kayak and parachute

**WHY IT'S WEIRD:**
Skyakers ride the air **instead of** white-water **rapids,** free-falling for some 8,000 feet (2400 m) before opening a parachute and **targeting** a **water** landing.

# Globe Riding

›

**SPECIAL GEAR:**
globe ball

**WHY IT'S WEIRD:**
Like a **hamster** inside its wheel, a globe rider runs inside a giant **inflated** ball cushioned with a layer of air as it **rolls** across water or down a steep hillside.

# Mountain Unicycling

‹‹‹

**SPECIAL GEAR:**
unicycle with extra-wide, knobby tires

**WHY IT'S WEIRD:**
Cyclists **climb** boulders, teeter on rocky ledges, and pedal through streams on one wheel—with **no brakes!**

# SpaceVacation

TAKING A **SPACE-CATION** WILL BE POSSIBLE IN YOUR LIFETIME. HERE ARE SOME WEIRD THINGS TO LOOK FORWARD TO AT YOUR ORBITAL RESORT:

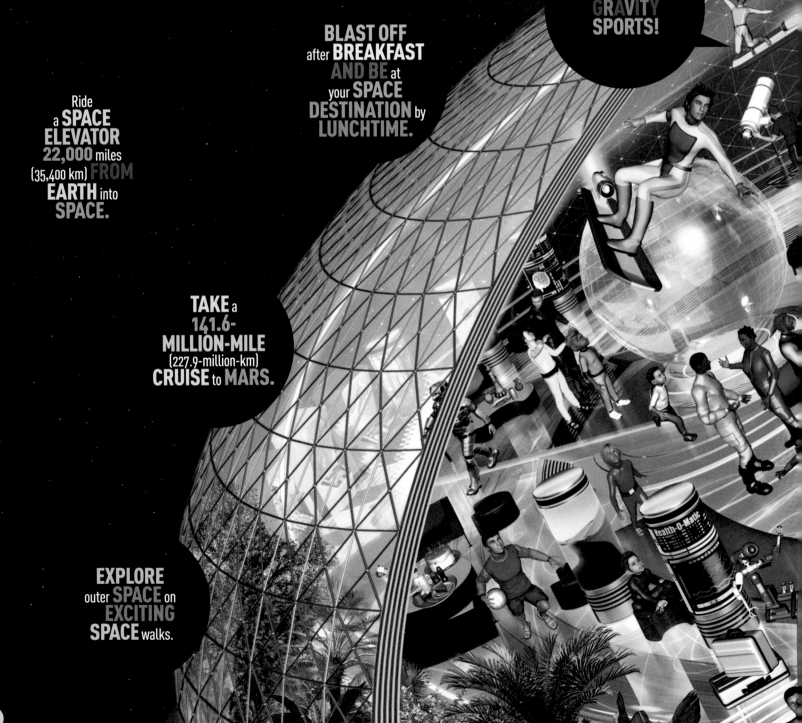

WATCH the **EVER-CHANGING** view of **EARTH** as the **HOTEL ROTATES** around it every **90** minutes.

Play **ZERO-GRAVITY SPORTS!**

**BLAST OFF** after **BREAKFAST AND BE** at your **SPACE DESTINATION** by **LUNCHTIME.**

Ride a **SPACE ELEVATOR 22,000** miles (35,400 km) **FROM EARTH** into **SPACE.**

**TAKE** a **141.6-MILLION-MILE** (227.9-million-km) **CRUISE** to **MARS.**

**EXPLORE** outer **SPACE** on **EXCITING SPACE** walks.

ENJOY a CLOSE-UP VIEW of the STARS.

Have FUN DODGING blobs of FLYING WATER in the WATER ROOM attraction.

WATER WORLD

ROBOTS help TAKE CARE of GUESTS' NEEDS.

AFRAID OF FLYING? Travel anywhere in the universe without LEAVING HOME with the latest HOLOGRAPHIC VACATION app.

# GREEN Extremes

## Air Pod

This tiny car runs on compressed air rather than fuel and weighs only as much as four 12-year-olds.

**THESE OVER-THE-TOP IDEAS** TAKE **ECO-FRIENDLY** TO A WHOLE NEW LEVEL. FIND OUT HOW FAR SOME PEOPLE WILL GO TO **REDUCE**, **REUSE**, AND **RECYCLE**.

>>>

## Solar Flight

On a long summer day, this solar-powered plane flew for more than 26 hours and reached a height of more than 5 miles (8.5 km), using only energy from the sun.

<<<

## Energy Boost

At a hotel in Denmark, guests can eat a free meal if they ride a stationary bike for 15 minutes, producing 10 watts of energy to help power the building.

## Cave Dwelling

This house was built inside a cave to save energy—the temperature stays the same year-round.

<<<

## Walking House

This house stores rainwater and runs on wind and solar power—and if your neighbors are noisy, it can *walk* to a new location!

>>>

## Pooch Power

A public dog park in Massachusetts, U.S.A., was the first to use a street lamp powered by the dogs' droppings!

## Bottle Boat

To raise awareness about smarter use of plastic waste, a crew sailed from California, U.S.A., to Sydney, Australia, in a boat made from 12,500 plastic bottles!

# ON THE EDGE

THE 2,345-FOOT (715-M)-TALL KJERAG WATERFALL IS ONE OF THE TALLEST IN THE WORLD.

MORE THAN 33,000 BASE JUMPS HAVE BEEN MADE FROM KJERAG PLATEAU.

IT'S A STEEP THREE-HOUR HIKE TO REACH THIS SPOT.

KJERAGBOLTEN IS ABOUT 6.5 FEET (2 M) ACROSS—AS WIDE AS THREE PEOPLE STANDING SIDE BY SIDE.

THE UNITARD WAS FIRST WORN BY SWIMMER AND ACTRESS ANNETTE KELLERMAN IN 1905.

DARING HIKERS OFTEN WALK ACROSS THIS BOULDER.

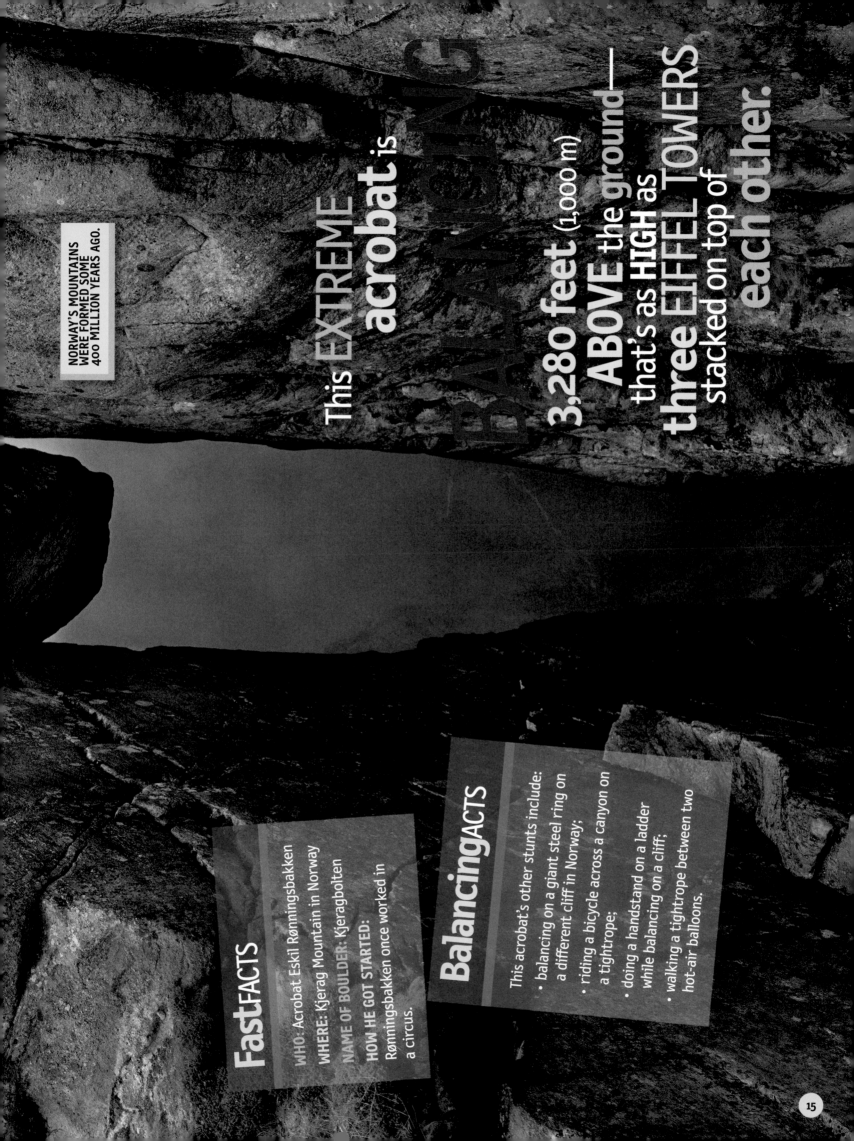

This EXTREME acrobat is

BALANCING

3,280 feet (1,000 m) ABOVE the ground— that's as HIGH as three EIFFEL TOWERS stacked on top of each other.

## FastFACTS

**WHO:** Acrobat Eskil Rønningsbakken

**WHERE:** Kjerag Mountain in Norway

**NAME OF BOULDER:** Kjeragbolten

**HOW HE GOT STARTED:** Rønningsbakken once worked in a circus.

## BalancingACTS

This acrobat's other stunts include:

• balancing on a giant steel ring on a different cliff in Norway;

• riding a bicycle across a canyon on a tightrope;

• doing a handstand on a ladder while balancing on a cliff;

• walking a tightrope between two hot-air balloons.

# WHICH IS HOTTER?

A KERNEL OF **POPCORN** WHEN IT POPS **356°F** (180°C)

THE TEMPERATURE A **SIDEWALK** MUST BE TO **FRY** **AN EGG** **158°F** (70°C)

WINNER!

**MARS** AT NIGHT **-200°F** (-130°C)

OUTSIDE AN AIRPLANE AT 30,000 FEET (9,144 M) **-49°F** (-45°C)

BOILING **WATER** TURNING TO **ICE** IN MIDAIR **-63°F** (-53°C)

THE
TEMPERATURE **LAVA**
CAN REACH
2,140°F
(1,170°C)

THE CENTER
OF A **CANDLE FLAME**
700°F
(370°C)

WINNER!

THE **SUN'S** CORE
27,000,000°F
(15,000,000°C)

ICEBERG
5 TO -4°F
(-15 TO -20°C)

ICE CREAM
3.2°F
(-16°C)

{ WHICH IS COLDER?

# REAL-LIFE SPiDER-MAN

HE HAS HAD TWO SERIOUS FALLS AND BROKEN MULTIPLE BONES.

ROBERT HAS VERTIGO—A CONDITION THAT CAUSES THE FEELING THAT YOU OR YOUR SURROUNDINGS ARE MOVING.

This daredevil, known as the **FRENCH SPIDER-MAN,** climbed for six hours to reach the top of the **WORLD'S TALLEST** skyscraper!

IT TOOK ROBERT ABOUT SIX HOURS TO CLIMB TO THE TOP.

THIS SKYSCRAPER, CALLED THE BURJ KHALIFA, HAS MORE THAN 160 STORIES!

THE ELEVATORS INSIDE THIS BUILDING TRAVEL FARTHER THAN ANY OTHERS IN THE WORLD.

THE FIRST URBAN CLIMBER, HARRY H. GARDINER, CLIMBED MORE THAN 700 BUILDINGS IN THE EARLY 1900s.

## Fast FACTS

**CLIMBER'S NAME:** Alain Robert

**TALLEST SKYSCRAPER:** Burj Khalifa

**WHERE:** Dubai, United Arab Emirates

**HOW TALL:** 2,717 feet (828 m)

**DON'T TRY THIS AT HOME:** It is illegal to climb buildings in many places. Robert sometimes gets arrested after his climbs.

*BUILDERING* IS ANOTHER NAME FOR THIS SPORT.

## Motoring Mouse >>>

**NAME: Bunsen**

**WHY HE'S AWESOME:**
Bunsen plays **captain** aboard
his boat, which his owner
**navigates** by remote control.

**FUN FACT:**
More than **two million** people
have also watched him surf on YouTube.

# Awesome ANiMALS in Action!

**NAME: Patch**

**WHY HE'S AWESOME:**
Patch **soars** 2,500 feet (762 m) in the
**air**—as high as a **250-story** building.

**FUN FACT:**
Patch also likes riding a
**motorcycle** with his owner.

## Flying Dog

## Scootering Macaw

**NAME: Zachary**

**WHY HE'S AWESOME:**
He likes riding his scooter almost as much as **flying.**

**FUN FACT:**
Zachary also **skateboards** and **rides a bike**
on a **high wire.**

## Surfer Cat

**NAME: Ice Breaker**

**WHY HE'S AWESOME:**
This cool cat **loves** the water. He **catches waves** at a beach in Florida, U.S.A.

**FUN FACT:**
When he's not surfing, Ice Breaker is at home **playing** in the **shower.**

**NAME: Albert Einstein**

**WHY HE'S AWESOME:**
This "**fintastic**" goldfish dribbles the ball with his **mouth**—and SCORES!

**FUN FACT:**
Albert also does the limbo, **plays football**, swims through a hoop, and **starred** in a **TV commercial!**

## Go-al Fish!

**NAME: ROSE**

**WHY SHE'S AWESOME:**
Rose **shreds** the bunny **slopes** at a ski resort near Los Angeles, California, U.S.A., with her bulldog **friend Tillman** (see page 6).

**FUN FACT:**
During a **parade** in Pasadena, California, Rose snowboarded on a specially designed **float.**

## Snowboarding Dog

A BLUE WHALE is almost as LOUD as a JET ENGINE (but you can't always hear it).

# A *2-inch (5-cm)* pistol shrimp is even LOUDER than a blue whale!

## ultimate secret revealed!

**There's no doubt about it: Blue whales are loudmouths.** But some of their vocals are too low for humans to hear. Humans can generally hear sounds as low as about 20 Hertz, but whales broadcast at 15 to 20 Hertz—or lower. These giants of the sea are solitary creatures, and scientists suspect their low vibrations help them communicate with other blue whales up to 300 miles (483 km) away. Now that's a long-distance call!

A **MAN** TREKKED 17,000 FEET (5,300 M) UP MOUNT EVEREST TO **SWIM** IN A LAKE, RAISING AWARENESS ABOUT CLIMATE CHANGE.

A TEAM OF **TORNADO CHASERS** BUILT A **14,000-POUND (6,350-KG)** VEHICLE THAT CAN DRiVE INTO TORNADOES WITH **WIND SPEEDS** UP TO **300** MILES AN HOUR (**483** KPH).

SOME **50** PEOPLE **SPEND THE WiNTER** AT THE **SOUTH POLE** EVERY YEAR.

A 16-YEAR-OLD GIRL SAiLED AROUND THE WORLD **NONSTOP BY HERSELF.**

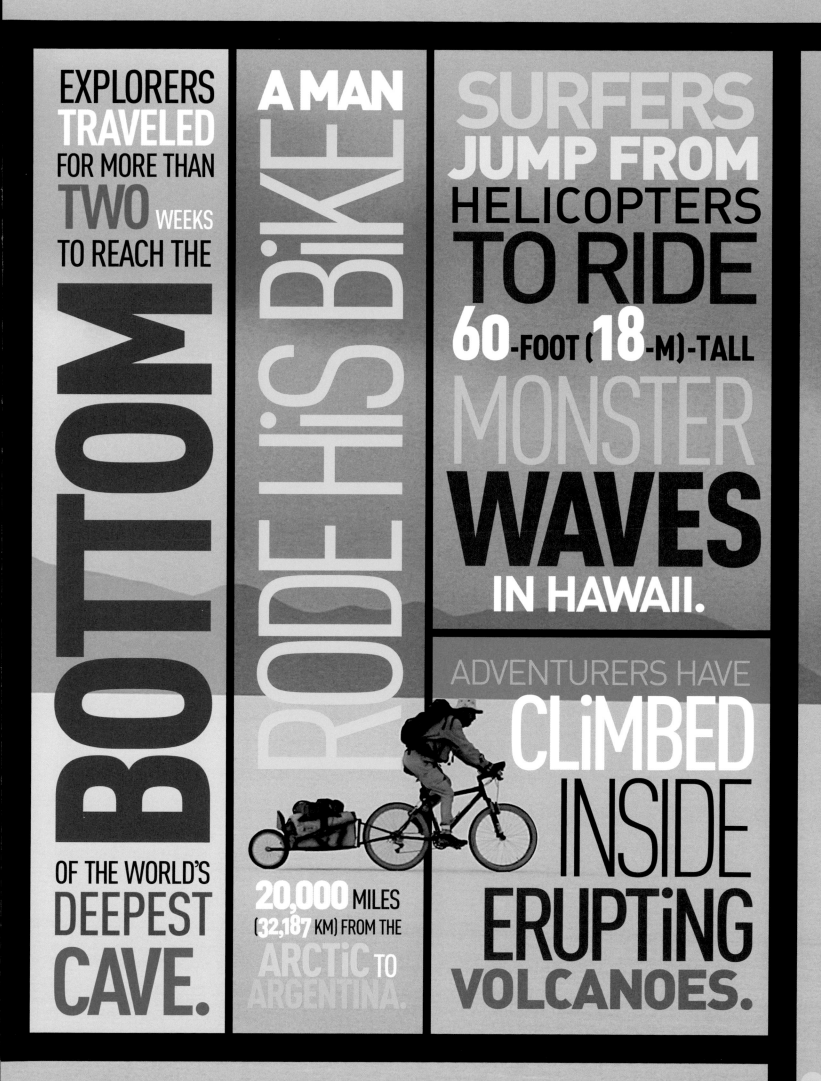

EXPLORERS TRAVELED FOR MORE THAN TWO WEEKS TO REACH THE BOTTOM OF THE WORLD'S DEEPEST CAVE.

A MAN RODE HIS BIKE 20,000 MILES (32,187 KM) FROM THE ARCTIC TO ARGENTINA.

SURFERS JUMP FROM HELICOPTERS TO RIDE 60-FOOT (18-M)-TALL MONSTER WAVES IN HAWAII.

ADVENTURERS HAVE CLIMBED INSIDE ERUPTING VOLCANOES.

**Tarsiers can't move their eyeballs.**

The Philippine tarsier has the biggest eyes relative to its size of any animal. This tiny primate—only three to six inches (8 to 15 cm) long, not including its tail—lives in the forest of southeastern Philippines. For more *eye*-popping facts, turn to page 40.

# CHAPTER 2

# Seeing iS Believing

## Reading Dog

**WHERE SHE LIVES:**
New York, New York, U.S.A.

**WHY SHE'S AMAZING:**
Willow the English terrier mix doesn't just **hear** her owner's commands—she also **reads** them. The pooch raises her paw when she sees the word **"wave"** and sits up when she sees the phrase **"sit up"**!

**WHERE HE LIVES:**
Cornwall, England, U.K.

**WHY HE'S AMAZING:**
Showing any kind of affection is **rare** for a reptile, but Timmy the tortoise has loved Tanya, the **plastic toy** tortoise, for **several years.** Who knows, maybe Tanya really brings Timmy out of his shell!

## Tortoise Friend

# AMAZING Animals

**WHERE SHE LIVES:**
Thirsk, England, U.K.

**WHY SHE'S AMAZING:**
Not all pigs love the **mud.** Cinders—who has a mysterious **fear** of dirt—wore doll-size boots to **protect** her, uh, little piggies from the muck.

## Pig in Boots

## Mother Hen

**WHERE SHE LIVES:**
Shrewsbury, England, U.K.

**WHY SHE'S AMAZING:**
When it comes to her **mothering** instincts, Mabel the hen clucks for pups! She looks after a litter of tiny **dogs** as if they are her own **chicks**—when their mom goes outside for a break, Mabel snuggles up and keeps the puppies toasty.

**WHERE HE LIVES:**
Spruce Grove, Alberta, Canada

**WHY HE'S AMAZING:**
Forget hooves—Bailey Jr. the **bison** gets around in the comforts of a **car.** To make room for this mammoth mammal, his owner removed the roof and front and rear passenger seats of a four-door car and **reinforced** the bottom. Now that's what you call **riding** in style!

## Backseat Bison

## Bionic Cat

**WHERE HE LIVES:**
Surrey, England, U.K.

**WHY HE'S AMAZING:**
After losing his **back paws** in an accident, doctors fit Oscar with the **first-ever** realistic cat paws. Oscar can now jump on beds, crawl up curtains, and even scratch his ears with his **plastic feet.** Hope there aren't any mice in this house!

## Musical Walrus

**WHERE SHE LIVES:**
Istanbul, Turkey

**WHY SHE'S AMAZING:**
Sara pretends to **play** a toy sax while **swaying** along to jazz music and flapping her flippers to the **beat.** That's one rockin' walrus!

# BASILISK LIZARDS

## are the only lizards that run on water.

→ Basilisks can stay underwater for 30 minutes.

→ Basilisks **live** mostly in the **rain forests** of Central and South America.

→ These lizards can **run** on water for more than **15 feet** (4.5 m) before dropping to all fours and swimming.

→ What makes a basilisk **defy gravity?** Large feet, widespread toes, and the ability to **windmill** its hind legs and feet so fast that it creates a **tiny air pocket** to keep it from sinking.

→ Baby basilisks can **climb, swim, and run** on land and water as soon as they **hatch.**

# SHAPE-SHIFTERS

Check out these totally wild animal transformations!

## LOVEBIRDS

**WHAT IT IS:** frigate bird

**WHERE IT LIVES:** tropical ocean coastlines

**EXTREME MAKEOVER:**
When trying to attract a female, the male inflates a heart-shaped sac that's half the size of the bird's body!

## STOP, DROP, AND ROLL!

**WHAT IT IS:** three-banded armadillo

**WHERE IT LIVES:** South America

**EXTREME MAKEOVER:**
Sensing danger, this stocky mammal ducks into its armorlike shell and rolls up into a predator-proof ball.

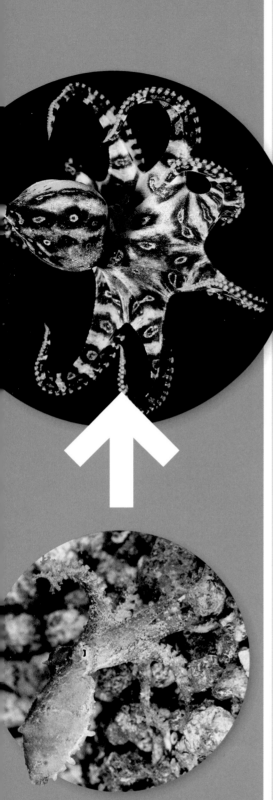

## LIGHT SHOW

**WHAT IT IS:** blue-ringed octopus

**WHERE IT LIVES:** warm, shallow waters off the coasts of Asia and Australia

**EXTREME MAKEOVER:**
Don't make this octopus angry! It will light up with electric blue rings in warning, and its bite is venomous enough to kill a human.

**WHAT IT IS:** flying squirrel

**WHERE IT LIVES:** forests of North America and Central America

**EXTREME MAKEOVER:**
These strange squirrels look normal until they spread out winglike skin flaps and soar from tree to tree. They don't really fly, but they can glide more than 150 feet (45 m).

## FISH BALL

**WHAT IT IS:** pufferfish

**WHERE IT LIVES:** tropical ocean waters; some species in freshwater

**EXTREME MAKEOVER:**
Predators beware! When this petite fish gets scared, it gulps down enough water to balloon to twice its size and then sticks out its prickly spines.

# ALL THAT glitters

THIS **CUPCAKE** IS SPRINKLED WITH AROUND **25 KARATS OF DIAMONDS** AND COSTS MORE THAN **$150,000**— ABOUT AS MUCH AS **FIVE CARS.**

>>> SOME HIGH-END **SPAS** OFFER **$500 MUD MASKS** MADE WITH **24-KARAT GOLD.**

INSTEAD OF **MONEY,** THIS "CASH" MACHINE IN ABU DHABI, UNITED ARAB EMIRATES, DISPENSES **24-KARAT GOLD BARS** AND **COINS.**

>>>

GOLD to go®
The gold ATM

Call button

**BEDAZZLED** WITH **300,000 CRYSTALS**, THIS **MERCEDES-BENZ** IS WORTH **$1 MILLION.** >>>

**"POTTY"** LIKE A **ROCK STAR** WITH A **SOLID-GOLD** TOILET <<< WORTH ABOUT **$37 MILLION.**

THIS **$70,000** TEDDY BEAR HAS DIAMOND-AND-SAPPHIRE EYES, >>> GOLD LEAF IN ITS **FUR**, AND A **24-KARAT** GOLD NOSE!

36

IT TAKES ABOUT

# 10 HOURS

FOR CHINESE

## ARTIST

### LIU BOLIN TO

## "DISAPPEAR"

INTO A

## SCENE.

BOLIN HAS ALSO **VANISHED** INTO THE **GREAT WALL** OF CHINA AND A LONDON **PHONE BOOTH,** AMONG OTHER PLACES.

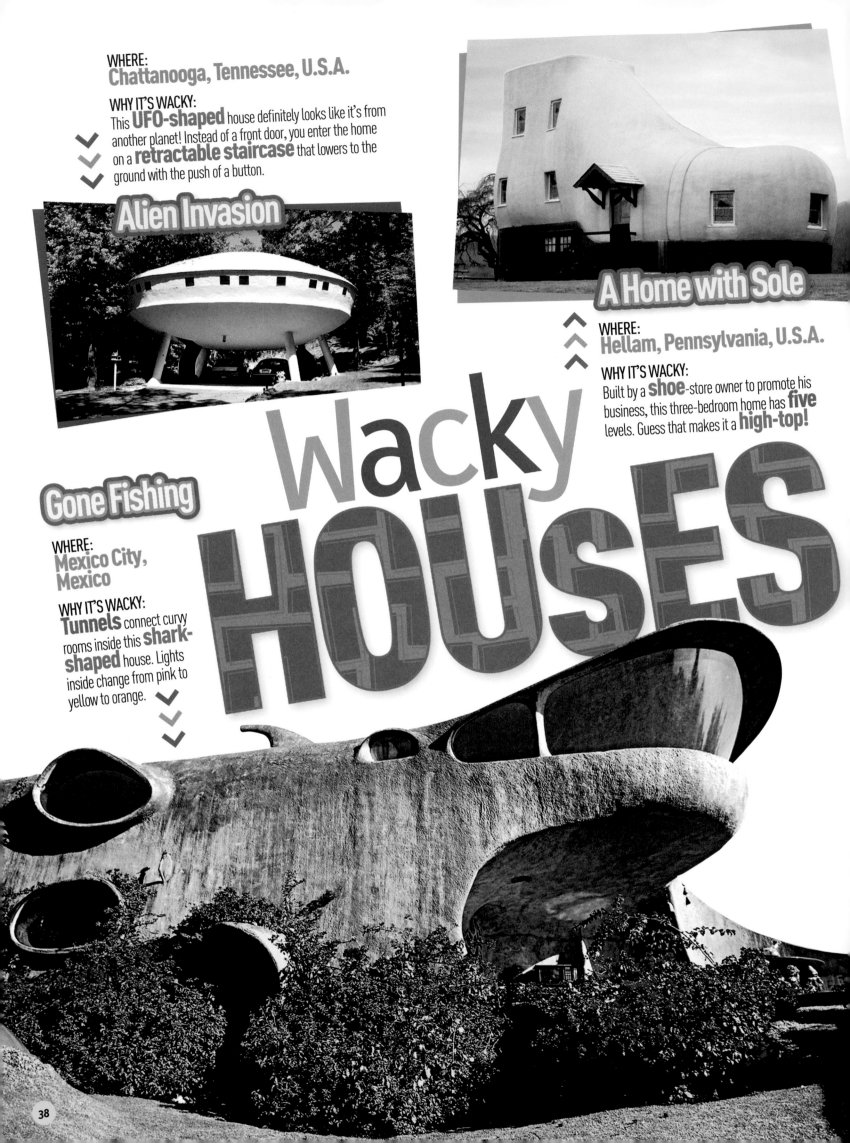

**WHERE:**
Chattanooga, Tennessee, U.S.A.

**WHY IT'S WACKY:**
This **UFO-shaped** house definitely looks like it's from another planet! Instead of a front door, you enter the home on a **retractable staircase** that lowers to the ground with the push of a button.

## Alien Invasion

## A Home with Sole

**WHERE:**
Hellam, Pennsylvania, U.S.A.

**WHY IT'S WACKY:**
Built by a **shoe**-store owner to promote his business, this three-bedroom home has **five** levels. Guess that makes it a **high-top!**

# Wacky HOUSES

## Gone Fishing

**WHERE:**
Mexico City, Mexico

**WHY IT'S WACKY:**
**Tunnels** connect curvy rooms inside this **shark-shaped** house. Lights inside change from pink to yellow to orange.

**WHERE:**
Salzburg, Austria

**WHY IT'S WACKY:**
This **car-shaped** house, a tribute to the original Volkswagen Beetle, features **headlight-shaped** windows and giant "tires" on the outside. The architect who built the house also built a VW-shaped restaurant!

>>>

## CARchitecture

**WHERE:**
Olympia, Washington, U.S.A.

**WHY IT'S WACKY:**
Talk about living the **high** life: This two-level tree house—spread out across **seven** trees—has its own **electricity** and heat!

## Up a Tree

## Rock On

**WHERE:**
Brittany, France

**WHY IT'S WACKY:**
Squeezed between **two boulders,** this tiny stone house was built in **1755** and was once a home for a **village fisherman.**

## Flipped Out

>>>

**WHERE:**
Trassenheide, Germany

**WHY IT'S WACKY:**
No wonder tons of tourists **flip** for this house: **Everything** is upside-down inside—including the **toilet!**

# 11 EYE-POPPING

**GOLDFISH CAN'T CLOSE THEIR EYES.**

**A squid's eyes** are each about the size of a **watermelon.**

**CHAMELEONS CAN SEE IN TWO DIFFERENT DIRECTIONS AT THE SAME TIME.**

YOU **BLINK** MORE THAN **10,000** TIMES A DAY.

Ostriches' eyes are **bigger** than their brains.

# FACTS

Some people can **HEAR** THEIR **EYEBALLS** MOVING.

**YOU CAN GET A** SUNBURN **ON YOUR EYES.**

A BUTTERFLY CAN SEE **ULTRAVIOLET** LIGHT.

DOLPHINS **SLEEP** WITH ONE EYE **OPEN.**

THE **HUMAN EYEBALL** WEIGHS ABOUT AS MUCH AS **FIVE QUARTERS.**

THE BLINK OF AN EYE **EQUALS** ABOUT TWO-FIFTHS OF A SECOND.

# FaNTASY ISLaND

THE TOTAL AMOUNT OF ROCKS AND SAND USED TO BUILD THE PALM ISLAND COULD FORM A 6-FOOT-TALL (2-M) WALL LONG ENOUGH TO CIRCLE THE GLOBE THREE TIMES.

THERE'S A MONORAIL TRAIN THAT TRANSPORTS PEOPLE FROM THE ISLAND'S "TRUNK" TO THE CRESCENT.

SOME YEARS, IT NEVER RAINS ON THE PALM JUMEIRAH.

28 BOTTLENOSE DOLPHINS WERE FLOWN FROM THE SOLOMON ISLANDS TO FILL DOLPHIN BAY, AN 11-ACRE LAGOON ON THE PALM'S CRESCENT.

THE 7-MILE (11-KM) CRESCENT SURROUNDING THE ISLAND IS MADE FROM MORE THAN 7 MILLION TONS OF ROCKS.

# This massive palm-tree-shaped island can be seen from the International Space Station, some 220 miles (354 km) above Earth!

## FastFACTS

**NAME:** The Palm Jumeirah

**WHAT:** One of three man-made islands in the Arabian Gulf that are shaped like palm trees!

**WHERE:** Dubai, United Arab Emirates

**SIZE:** 12 square miles (31 sq km)—as big as 5,800 football fields

**COST TO BUILD:** $12 billion

A LUXURY VILLA ON ONE OF THE ISLAND'S "FRONDS" SELLS FOR ABOUT $5 MILLION.

## ISLANDS TAKE SHAPE

**FEDERATION ISLAND** This yet-to-be-built island in the Black Sea will look like a map of Russia.

**THE WORLD** This collection of 300 man-made islands in Dubai is shaped like a world map and cost $14 billion ($14,000,000,000) to build.

**GALESNJAK** This tiny natural island in the Adriatic Sea off the coast of Croatia is perfectly heart shaped.

THERE ARE ENOUGH HOMES AND HOTEL ROOMS ON THE ISLAND TO FIT 65,000 PEOPLE.

# CRAZY ArT

ARTISTS MADE A
**10-FOOT** (3-m)
**HOT DOG**
USING
**6,300** CANS OF
BAKED BEANS,
VIENNA SAUSAGES,
AND MORE.

THIS **10-FOOT-TALL** (3-m)
**BALLOON DOG**—ACTUALLY
COLORED STAINLESS
STEEL—
IS FEATURED IN
THE MOVIE
*NIGHT AT THE MUSEUM 2.*

BALLOON DOG BY JEFF

A **DUTCH**
ARTIST SPENT TWO DAYS
**SPRAY-PAINTING**
GIANT FRIED **EGGS**
ON A LARGE CITY SQUARE.

THIS **TIGER** IS SCULPTED ENTIRELY FROM **SUGAR.** THE ART OF SUGAR SCULPTURE BEGAN IN **CHINA** MORE THAN **500** YEARS AGO.

THE BIGGEST **SNOW SCULPTURES, LIKE THESE DINOS, CAN** WEIGH UP TO **100 TONS** (90 t) THAT'S MORE THAN **30** HIPPOS.

THE ART OF CREATING **IMAGES** OUT OF RUBIK'S CUBES, LIKE THIS **PAC-MAN GHOST,** IS CALLED **RUBIK'S CUBISM.**

White **rhinos** can thunder through brush at **28 miles** an hour (45 kph).

All five types of rhinos have at least one horn, excellent hearing, and a fancy for rolling in the mud. Find out what weighs as much as 160 million rhinos on page 55.

# CHAPTER 3

# WHO'S COUNTING?

Scientists have **determined** that every animal **pictured** here has at least a basic **ability** to count.

## Chickens

**Baby** chicks have been shown to have an **inborn** sense of numbers and can **perform** simple addition and subtraction.

<<<

# Counting CRiTTERS

## Honeybees

In exchange for a **sweet** treat, bees can learn to **distinguish** among patterns containing 2, 3, and 4 dots.

## Red-Backed Salamander

When given the choice among **fruit fly-filled** tubes, these salamanders could tell the **difference** among 1, 2, and 3 flies.

# Rhesus Monkeys

These primates show a number sense that's similar to our own. In some computer tests, researchers found that rhesus monkeys and college students earned similar results.

<<<

These finned math whizzes can tell the difference among groups of 1 to 4 fish.

vvv

# Mosquito Fish

# American Coots

These birds tally the number of eggs they lay in their nests. When an invading bird tries to sneak an egg in, the coot knows there's an extra and rejects it.

>>>

In tests, lemurs can put groups of dots in order according to number.

# Ring-tailed Lemurs

<<<

→ The first sharks appeared
**40 million** years before Earth's first trees.

→ A shark can detect a fish's **heartbeat**
up to 3 feet (0.9 m) away.

→ Sharks have
zero **bones.**

→ A shark can grow and
lose up to **30,000**
teeth in a lifetime.

**6 weeks** → A shark can live up to
without eating.

# A GREAT WHITE SHARK
## can weigh as much as
## 15 gorillas.

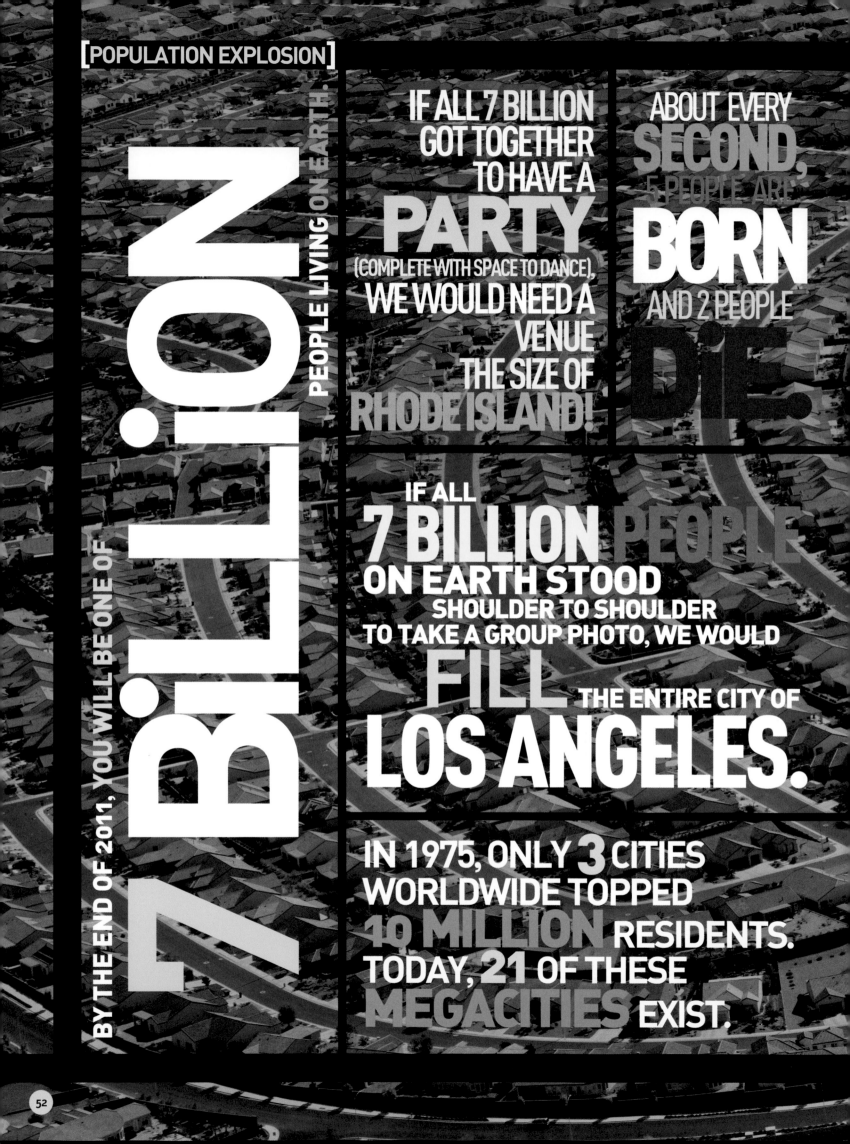

BY THE END OF 2011, YOU WILL BE ONE OF

7 BILLION

PEOPLE LIVING ON EARTH.

IF ALL 7 BILLION GOT TOGETHER TO HAVE A **PARTY** (COMPLETE WITH SPACE TO DANCE), WE WOULD NEED A VENUE THE SIZE OF RHODE ISLAND!

ABOUT EVERY **SECOND,** 5 PEOPLE ARE **BORN** AND 2 PEOPLE **DIE.**

IF ALL **7 BILLION** PEOPLE ON EARTH STOOD SHOULDER TO SHOULDER TO TAKE A GROUP PHOTO, WE WOULD **FILL** THE ENTIRE CITY OF **LOS ANGELES.**

IN 1975, ONLY **3** CITIES WORLDWIDE TOPPED **10 MILLION** RESIDENTS. TODAY, **21** OF THESE MEGACITIES EXIST.

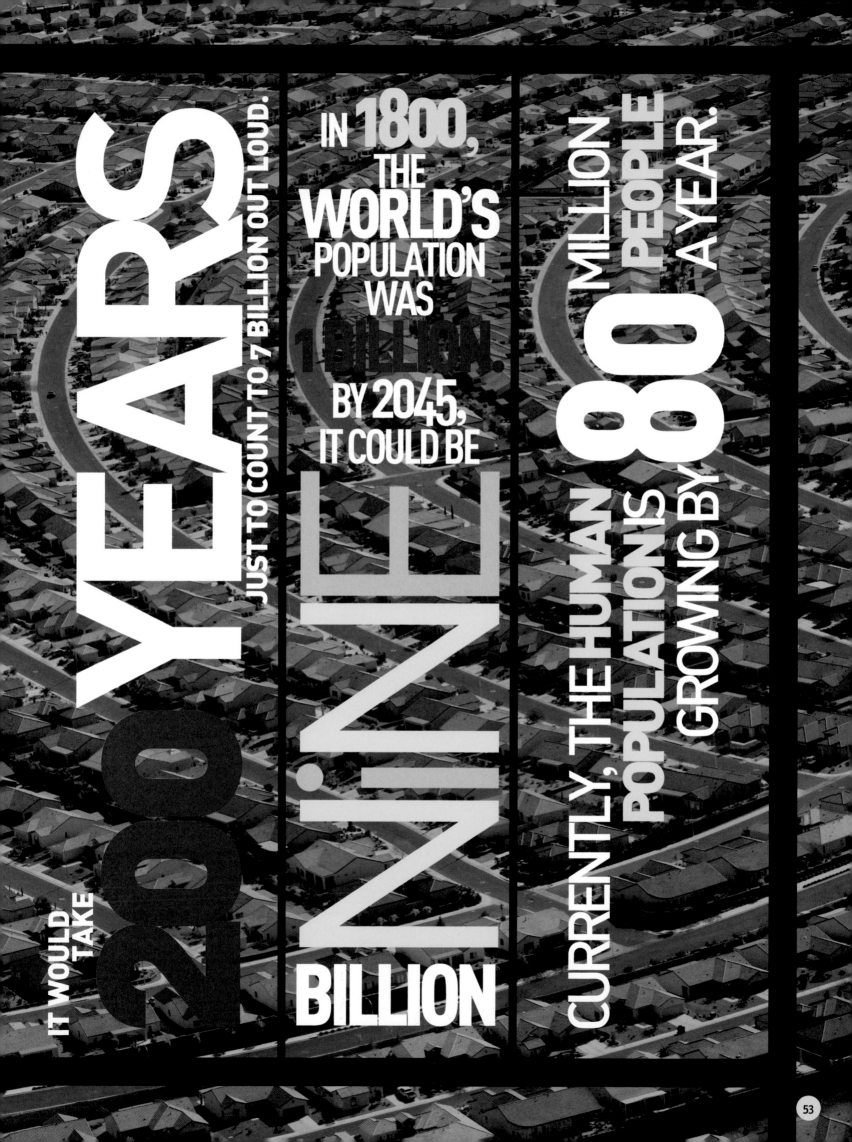

IT WOULD TAKE **200 YEARS**

JUST TO COUNT TO 7 BILLION OUT LOUD.

IN **1800**, THE **WORLD'S** POPULATION WAS **1 BILLION.** BY 2045, IT COULD BE **NINE BILLION**

CURRENTLY, THE HUMAN POPULATION IS GROWING BY **80** MILLION PEOPLE A YEAR.

# Storm
# WARNING!

(1  = 320,000 rhinos)

# A hurricane weighs as much as 160 million rhinos.

## **Fast**FACTS

A hurricane can weigh 100 billion pounds (454 million kg) —that's the same as 160 million rhinos.

A storm cloud weighs as much as 24 million rhinos.

A hurricane is also known as a typhoon or a cyclone depending on where in the world it forms.

Hurricanes can unleash more than 2.4 trillion gallons (9.1 trillion l) of rain a day.

The largest land animal that ever lived was a hornless rhinoceros called *Indricotherium*. It lived 30 million years ago, weighed at least 15 tons (13.6 t), and was as tall as a modern-day giraffe.

# WHICH
## ONE HAS THE
# LONGEST LEAP?

IMPALA
**36** FEET (11 M)

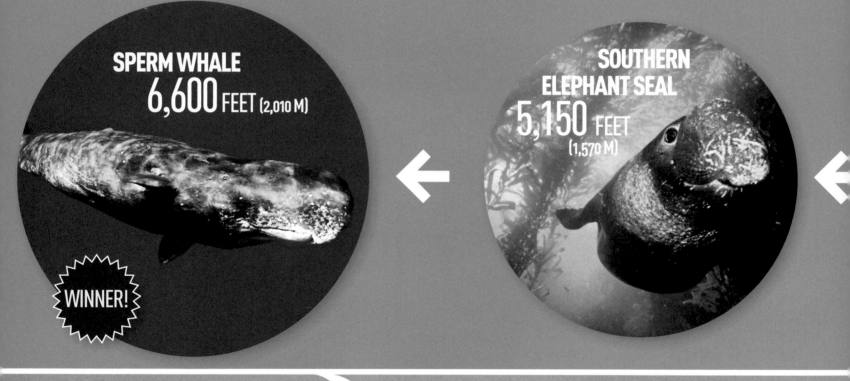

SPERM WHALE
**6,600** FEET (2,010 M)

**WINNER!**

SOUTHERN
ELEPHANT SEAL
**5,150** FEET
(1,570 M)

CHOMP WARS

# WHICH
## ONE HAS THE
# STRONGEST BITE?

DOG
**164** POUNDS (74 KG)
OF FORCE

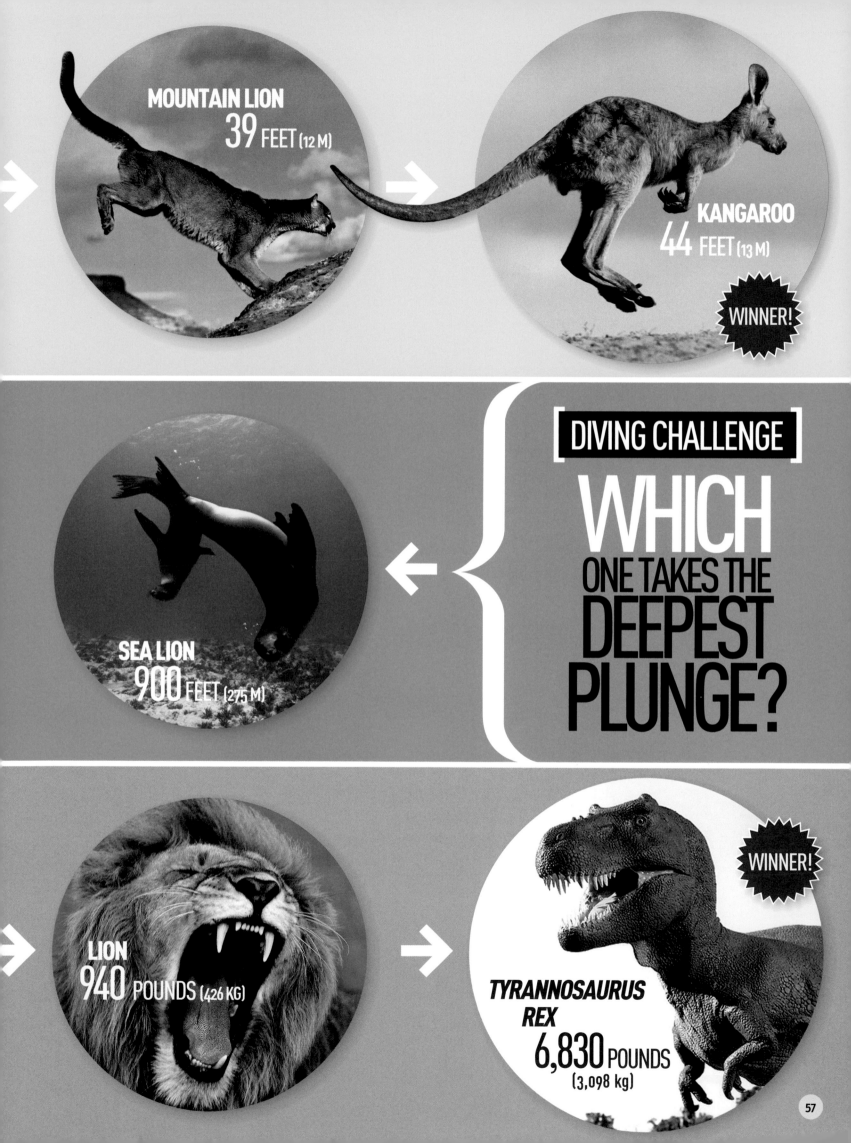

**MOUNTAIN LION**
39 FEET (12 M)

**KANGAROO**
44 FEET (13 M)

**WINNER!**

**[ DIVING CHALLENGE ]**

# WHICH
## ONE TAKES THE
# DEEPEST
# PLUNGE?

**SEA LION**
900 FEET (275 M)

**LION**
940 POUNDS (426 KG)

**WINNER!**

**TYRANNOSAURUS REX**
6,830 POUNDS (3,098 kg)

# 8 Cool Facts ABOUT

NAKED **MOLE RATS** LIVE ALMOST **TEN TIMES** LONGER THAN THEIR **MOUSE** OR STREET **RAT** COUSINS.
(THEIR SECRET: THEY APPARENTLY NEVER GET CANCER.)

A GALÁPAGOS TORTOISE IN AN AUSTRALIAN ZOO LIVED TO BE ABOUT **175** YEARS OLD.

A FRENCH WOMAN HAD THE **LONGEST** DOCUMENTED **LIFE SPAN** EVER RECORDED. SHE LIVED FOR **122** YEARS AND **164** DAYS.

# LiFE SPANS

A **405**-YEAR-OLD **CLAM**

FOUND IN **2007** WAS **ALIVE** WHEN **SHAKESPEARE** WAS **WRITING** *MACBETH.*

THE GIANT SEQUOIA TREES OF CALIFORNIA'S **REDWOOD** **FORESTS** CAN LIVE FOR MORE THAN **3,000** YEARS.

TODAY THE AVERAGE PERSON LIVES **67** YEARS.

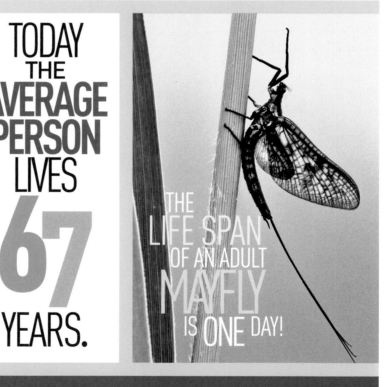

THE LIFE SPAN OF AN ADULT MAYFLY IS ONE DAY!

SCIENTISTS WERE **SHOCKED** TO FIND **STONE-TIPPED** HARPOONS FROM THE **1800s** IN SOME **BOWHEAD WHALES'** BODIES. NOW THEY BELIEVE THE WHALES CAN LIVE UP TO **200 YEARS.**

A **GIRAFFE** IS AS **TALL** **AS A STACK OF** **3** OSTRICHES, **9** KOALAS, OR **36** CHIPMUNKS.

CHIPMUNK = ½ FOOT [0.2 m]

KOALA = 2 FEET [0.6 m]

OSTRICH = 6 FEET [1.8 m]

GIRAFFE = 18 FEET [5.5 M]

61

# Time
## in the
# Tub

## FastFACTS

All the things you use, do, and eat in your lifetime add up. There are some other numbers that show an American's average human footprint—the mark you make on the Earth.

You'll drink 13,056 pints (6,178 liters) of milk.

You'll eat 4,476 loaves of bread.

You'll use 656 bars of soap and 198 bottles of shampoo.

You'll guzzle 43,371 cans of soda.

You'll spend $52,972 on clothes.

This parade of **28,433** rubber ducks represents the number of **showers** you'll take in your lifetime.

If humans had the metabolism of a hummingbird, we would need to eat about 400 a day.

# Some HUMMINGBIRDS consume up to 8 times their body weight in nectar each day.

**ultimate secret revealed!**

**Why would an animal that can be as small as a thumb need to pig out in such proportions?** Hummingbirds are the only birds that can hover like a helicopter or a bee. In order to achieve this aerial balancing act, they beat their flexible wings up to 200 times a second. This allows them to accomplish feats such as flying in one place, backward, and even upside down. Most importantly, hovering allows the birds to feed on the nectar of flowers. But because hummingbirds' in-flight aerobatics require so much energy, these tiny birds have big appetites to fuel.

An
**octopus**
has **3** hearts.

This 8-inch (20-cm) *Amphioctopus siamensis* was photographed off the coast of Papua New Guinea. It's one of more than 300 species of octopus living in oceans around the world. Read more weird animal facts on pages 74 and 75.

# CHAPTER 4

# FrEAKs oF NaTuRe

It *once*
# RAINED
# FROGS
in Kansas City, Missouri, U.S.A.

It has *also* RAINED worms, fish, toads, tadpoles, and birds in other places around the world.

(But, as far as we know, it has never rained cats and dogs!)

## ultimate secret revealed!

**Last time we checked, frogs couldn't fly.** But tornadoes and powerful storms sometimes vacuum up the surface of ponds, including frogs, fish, and other animals that live in and near the water. When the storm breaks up, the animals fall from the sky.

## TOOTHY TALLY

# WHICH
## HAS MORE
# TEETH?

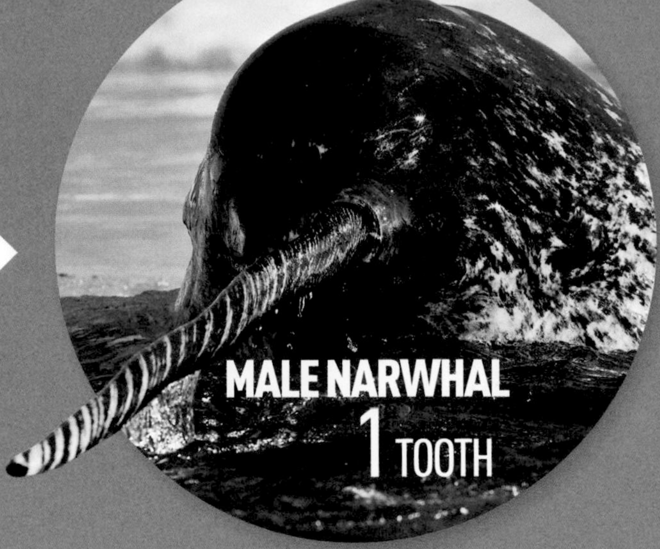

→

**MALE NARWHAL**
**1** TOOTH

**WINNER!**

**ELEPHANT**
CAN EAT **300** POUNDS
(136 KG) A DAY

←

**GORILLA**
CAN EAT **45** POUNDS
(20 KG) A DAY

←

## FUR-ST PLACE

# WHICH
## ONE IS
# HAIRIEST?

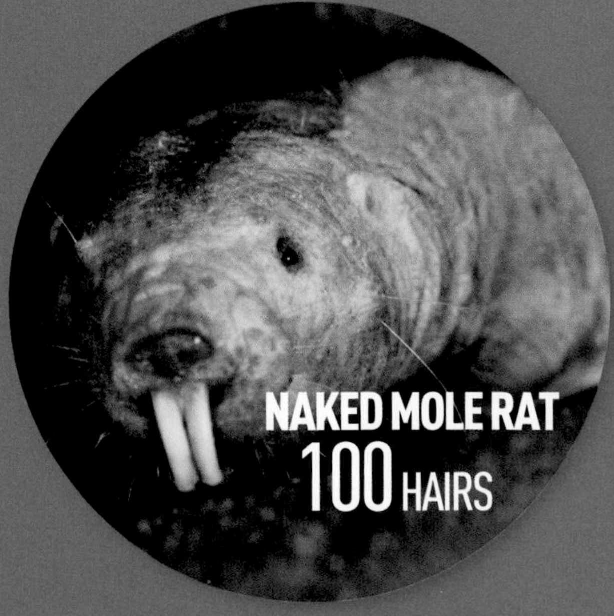

→

**NAKED MOLE RAT**
**100** HAIRS

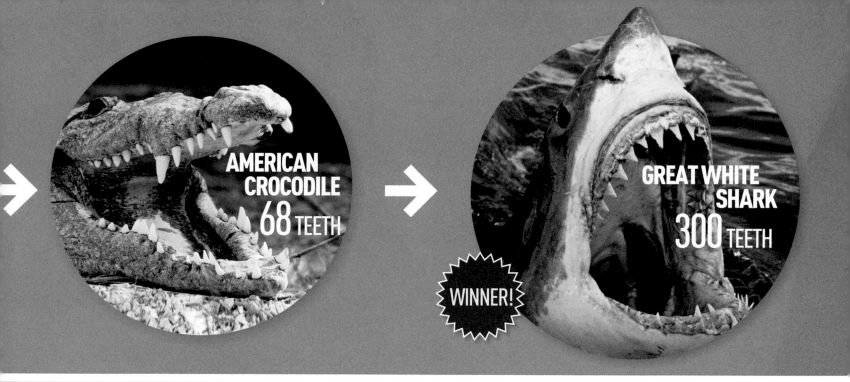

→ **AMERICAN CROCODILE** 68 TEETH

→ **GREAT WHITE SHARK** 300 TEETH

**WINNER!**

**LEOPARD** CAN EAT 7 POUNDS (3.6 KG) A DAY

←

**[ MEGA MUNCHERS ]**

# WHICH ONE EATS THE MOST?

→ **HUMAN HEAD** 100,000 HAIRS

→

**WINNER!**

**SEA OTTER** 800 MILLION HAIRS

# Over the Moon

**THESE AMAZING FACTS ABOUT THE MOON WILL MAKE YOU AS SMART AS A ROCKET SCIENTIST.**

A **100**-pound (45-kg) **PERSON WEIGHS** about **17** pounds (8 kg) on the **MOON.**

It's **IMPOSSIBLE** to **WHISTLE** on the **MOON.**

There is **NO WIND** or **SOUND** on the **MOON.**

**WITHOUT** a **SPACE SUIT,** an astronaut's **BLOOD** would **BOIL INSTANTLY.**

**JAMES B. IRWIN,** an astronaut on **APOLLO 15,** became the **EIGHTH** person to **WALK ON** the moon on **JULY 30,** **1971.**

The **LAST PERSON** to **STAND** on the moon was **THERE** in 1972.

More **PEOPLE** have **TRAVELED** to the **MOON** than to the **DEEPEST** part of the **OCEAN.**

APOLLO 15 ASTRONAUTS BLASTED back to the SPACECRAFT in the TOP of this LUNAR MODULE.

The MOON is moving 1.5 INCHES (3.8 cm) AWAY from EARTH every YEAR.

The BOTTOM of this LUNAR MODULE is STILL on the MOON.

The SURFACE of the MOON is SMALLER than ASIA.

APOLLO 15 astronauts DROVE this LUNAR ROVING VEHICLE a TOTAL of 17.5 MILES (28 km).

The MOON was likely CREATED when a CELESTIAL BODY the SIZE of MARS COLLIDED with EARTH!

It's a MYTH that PEOPLE act STRANGELY during a FULL MOON.

**WHERE IT LIVES:**
**in homes**

**WHY IT'S WEIRD:**
Born with almost **no fur,** these cats can cost as much as **$3,000.**

**Furless Cat**
<<<

# World's WEiRDEST Animals

**Liger**

**WHERE IT LIVES:**
**only in zoos**

**WHY IT'S WEIRD:**
This half lion, half tiger has a **lion's face** and a **tiger's stripes**—a big cat combo that would never occur in nature.

**Zedonk**
>>

**WHERE IT LIVES:**
**wildlife preserve**

**WHY IT'S WEIRD:**
Her mom is a **donkey,** and her dad is a **zebra.** The result? A donkey's brown **coat** on top and a zebra's **striped** legs.

## Star-nosed Mole

<<<

**WHERE IT LIVES:**
**North America**

**WHY IT'S WEIRD:**
Twenty-two pink **tentacles** on its **nose** help the mole feel its way around.

**WHERE IT LIVES:**
**aquariums only**

**WHY IT'S WEIRD:**
The fluid-filled sacs around its **eyes** are so **big** and **heavy** that the fish can barely lift its **head.**

## Bubble-eye Goldfish

## Proboscis Monkey

**WHERE IT LIVES:**
**Borneo**

**WHY IT'S WEIRD:**
A male's **nose** can be 7 inches (18 cm) long— as long as a pencil. Scientists think the supersized **schnoz** attracts females.

>>>

## Frilled Lizard

<<<

**WHERE IT LIVES:**
**Australia and New Guinea**

**WHY IT'S WEIRD:**
When this lizard gets freaked out, its hood **flares** out, its mouth opens **wide,** and it stands up on two back legs. Then it **sprints** for the nearest tree.

A **SHARK** COULD SMELL **A DROP** OF BLOOD IN A SWIMMING POOL.

**SWEET** FLAVORS.

CATS CANNOT TASTE

SOME **MOTHS** DROP FROM THE AIR WHEN THEY HEAR A **BAT** NEARBY.

**KIDS CAN HEAR SOUNDS** SOME ADULTS CANNOT.

THE NEARLY 9-FOOT (2.74-M)-TALL **CORPSE FLOWER** **SMELLS** LIKE **ROTTEN MEAT** AND WEIGHS **170** POUNDS (77 KG).

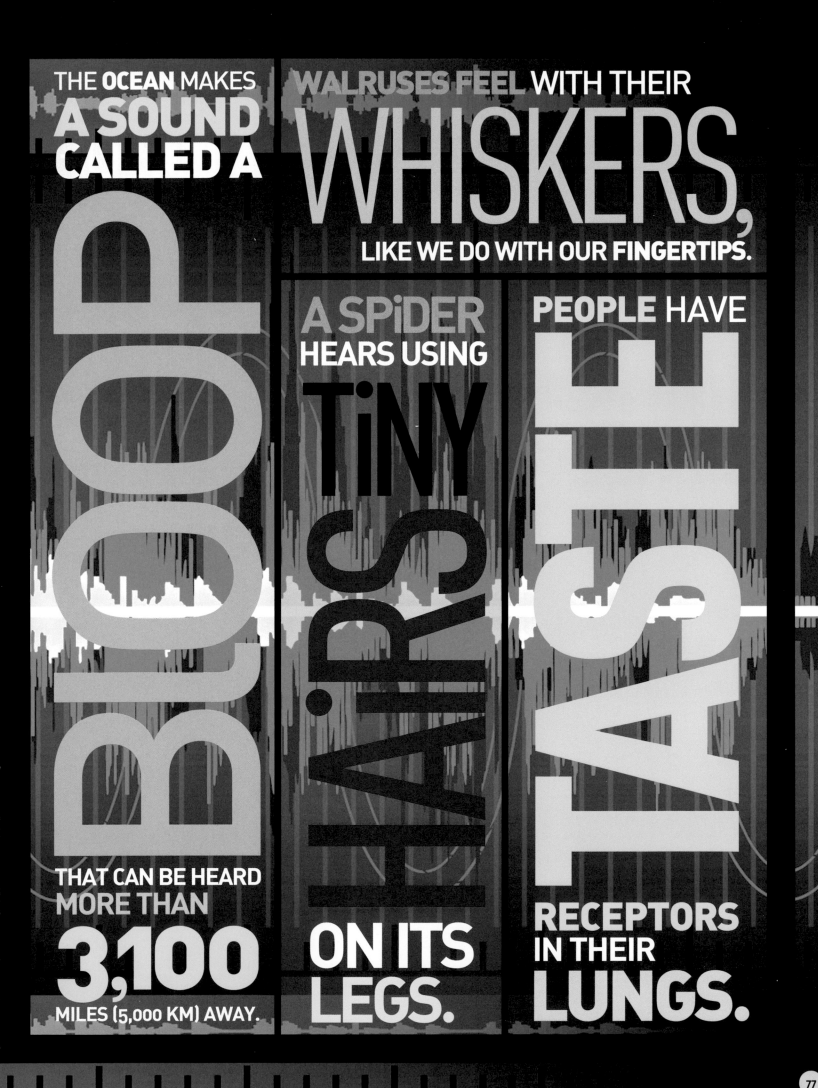

THE **OCEAN** MAKES. **A SOUND CALLED A**

# BLOOP

THAT CAN BE HEARD MORE THAN

## 3,100

MILES (5,000 KM) AWAY.

WALRUSES FEEL WITH THEIR

# WHISKERS,

LIKE WE DO WITH OUR **FINGERTIPS.**

A SPiDER HEARS USING **TiNY**

# HAiRS

ON ITS LEGS.

PEOPLE HAVE

# TASTE

RECEPTORS IN THEIR **LUNGS.**

You **DRINK** the same **WATER** as the dinosaurs!

You *also* **DRINK** the same water as woolly mammoths, the first humans, and King Tut.

**ultimate secret revealed!**

**Earth has been recycling water for more than four billion years.** Earth has no more or less water now than at any other time, including when George Washington, Cleopatra, or the dinosaurs were around. Water constantly evaporates from streams, rivers, and oceans into the sky. Some water even stays trapped in ice sheets. Rain, snow, and sleet bring evaporated water back to Earth. Then the whole process starts over again. So all of the water on Earth now has been here since Earth began.

# This LIGHTHOUSE turned into a giant ice sculpture during a WINTER STORM— and stayed that way for two weeks!

# DEEP FREEZE

## En-light-ening TRIVIA

WIND AND WAVES POUNDED AGAINST THE BUILDING, AND WATER FROZE AS IT HIT THE LIGHTHOUSE.

1. Sailors can hear the lighthouse's foghorn 12 miles (19 km) away and see its light from 10 miles (16 km) away.

2. The lighthouse operates on solar power.

3. The first lighthouse was built between 300 B.C. and 280 B.C. in Egypt.

THE LIGHT INSIDE WAS AUTOMATED IN 1965, SO THERE'S NO ONE INSIDE.

THIS IS THE FOG SIGNAL BUILDING.

CANADA IS 50 MILES (80 KM) NORTH.

THE LIGHTHOUSE IS ACCESSIBLE ONLY BY BOAT.

WHY IT'S FREAKY:
Snowballs **roll themselves.**

HOW IT HAPPENS: Strong **winds** can roll **snowballs** when new snow falls and can't stick to slippery ice underneath.

## Snow Rollers

<<<

# FREAKY Weather

WHY IT'S FREAKY:
Called **circumzenithal** arcs, these rainbows are **upside down!**

HOW IT HAPPENS:
They are usually seen in **colder** areas because they are caused by the refraction of light through **ice crystals** rather than raindrops.

## Confused Rainbows

## Super Tornado

WHY IT'S FREAKY:
With **winds of up to 300 miles** an hour (480 kph), these high-speed tornadoes are so destructive they can **rip pavement** off the streets and derail trains.

HOW IT HAPPENS:
Supercell **thunderstorms** sometimes spin into huge horizontal cyclones, called **mesocyclones.** If these spinning storms tip down and **touch down** on the ground, they become terrifying twisters!

## Tube-Shaped Clouds

**WHY IT'S FREAKY:**
Every year these **odd** clouds form over northern Australia and stretch for **620 miles** (1,000 km).

**HOW IT HAPPENS:**
The tube shape clouds form when a sea breeze **collides** with a shallow layer of **cold air.**

## Rogue Waves

**WHY IT'S FREAKY:**
**Ten-story-tall** waves form in the middle of the ocean, even in **mild weather** conditions.

**HOW IT HAPPENS:**
What causes a **freak wave** is a complete **mystery.**

## Fire Whirls

**WHY IT'S FREAKY:**
It's a **tornado** made of **fire!**

**HOW IT HAPPENS:**
When heat from a **wildfire** causes air to rise and fresh air swoops in, it can create a fire **tornado** that can be 50 feet [15 m] wide and **40 stories tall.**

## Grapefruit-size Hail

**WHY IT'S FREAKY:**
Giant hailstones **plummet** to Earth at about a hundred miles an hour (160 kph).

**HOW IT HAPPENS:**
Huge hail is created when updrafts carry raindrops as high as **50,000** feet (15,240 m). The **longer** the hail is carried by the wind, the more **ice crystals** it collects and the more **supersized** it becomes.

BOTTLENOSE DOLPHIN—
1,560 FEET (476 M)

A FLEA JUMPS more than 130 TIMES its height.

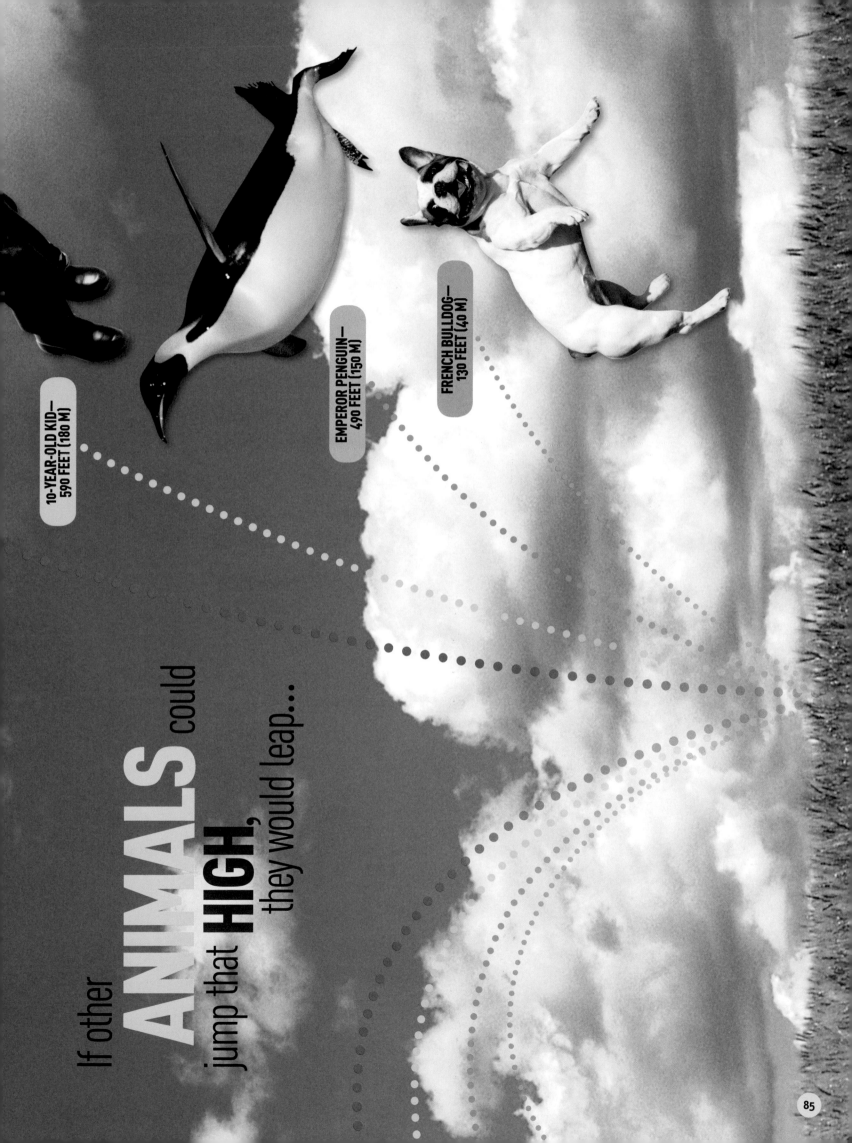

If other **ANIMALS** could jump that **HIGH,** they would leap...

10-YEAR-OLD KID—
590 FEET (180 M)

EMPEROR PENGUIN—
490 FEET (150 M)

FRENCH BULLDOG—
130 FEET (40 M)

**Cheetahs** can change direction in midair when chasing prey.

What's faster than a cheetah? Not much! The world's fastest land mammals, cheetahs live in parts of Africa and Iran. These cool cats have existed on Earth for about four million years! For more fast facts, turn to page 100.

# On the MoVE

# SiNK OR SWiM?

BUILT-IN BREATHING TANK

3 BATTERY-POWERED ENGINES:
1 FOR LAND
2 FOR UNDERWATER

SQUBA CAR IS A ZERO-EMISSION CAR.

This sQuba CAR can drive on land or underwater.

My scooter is 5x faster than your car!

## FastFACTS

NAME: sQuba car

COST: $1.75 million

MAX. LAND SPEED: 75 mph (120 kph)

MAX. WATER SURFACE SPEED: 4 mph (6 kph)

MAX. UNDERWATER SPEED: 1.8 mph (3 kph)

INSPIRED BY: aquatic car in the classic James Bond movie *The Spy Who Loved Me*

WHY A CONVERTIBLE? THE OPEN ROOF DOUBLES AS AN EMERGENCY EXIT!

INTERIOR DECORATED WITH MOTHER-OF-PEARL AND DIAMONDS

## HOW TO PASS A DRIVER'S TEST

1 Put on a breathing mask.

2 Buckle up to avoid floating away.

3 Drive into the ocean.

4 Open doors to let in water and begin to sink.

5 Accelerate, plunging 30 feet (9 m).

6 Adjust the thrust to make the car resurface.

7 Back on land? A laser system can drive the car. . . without a driver!

THIS **MOUSE** **HITCHED** A RIDE ON A **FROG'S** **BACK** TO ESCAPE A **FLOODED** **STREET** IN LUCKNOW, INDIA.

**FROGS DRINK** THROUGH THEIR **SKIN.**

WHEN **MICE** **SWIM** THEY USE THEIR **TAILS** LIKE MOTORS TO PROPEL THEM IN THE **WATER.**

**FROG BONES** GROW NEW **RINGS** AS THEY AGE, JUST LIKE **TREES.**

# FaSTer
# THAN THE SPEED OF SOUND

AS THE JET BREAKS THROUGH THE CLOUD, THE RELEASE OF AIR PRESSURE SENDS SHOCK WAVES TO THE GROUND, CAUSING A THUNDEROUS NOISE ALSO KNOWN AS A SONIC BOOM.

VFA-103

320

THE CLOUD IS A CLUSTER OF CONDENSATION THAT CAN FORM JUST AS THE JET BREAKS THE SOUND BARRIER.

SOUND TRAVELS MORE SLOWLY IN COLDER TEMPERATURES.

THE SPEED OF SOUND IS FASTER IN WATER THAN IN AIR.

TWO POWERFUL ENGINES HELP THIS JET REACH A TOP SPEED OF MACH 1.8—ALMOST TWICE THE SPEED OF SOUND.

WHEN AN OBJECT REACHES MACH 1, IT IS TRAVELING AT THE SPEED OF SOUND.

# This AIRCRAFT is breaking the SOUND BARRIER at 741 MILES an hour.

(1,193 kph)

## Full SPEED AHEAD

Space shuttles in orbit travel at around Mach 22—23.35 times the speed of sound.

A jet-powered car called the ThrustSSC can top 764 mph (1,229 kph)—slightly more than one percent faster than the speed of sound.

An airforce pilot came close to breaking the sound barrier when he skydived from 102,800 feet (31,333 m) above Earth at a speed of 614 mph (988 kph), or Mach 0.83.

# WeiRd WayS TO GET ArOUND

THIS DRIVABLE HIGH-HEELED **SHOE** IS MADE OUT OF SPARE **MOTORCYCLE PARTS.**

**FIFI,** THE 13-FOOT-TALL (4-m), 1,500-POUND (680-kg) **POODLE,** CAN TRAVEL ON LAND, WATER, AND THROUGH MUD.

THE **TOP BUN** OF THIS **"HAMBURGER HARLEY"** FLIPS OPEN FOR EASY ACCESS TO THE DRIVER'S **SEAT.**

A TEAM **PEDALED** **1,159.7 MILES** (1,866.4 km) IN **28 DAYS** ON THIS TRICYCLE BUILT FOR SEVEN.

>>> THE HORN OF THIS **"COWASAKI"** MOTORCYCLE MAKES A **MOOING** SOUND.

EVERY **PART** OF THIS **MONOWHEEL**— FROM THE HANDLEBARS TO THE ENGINE— SITS INSIDE A **GIANT WHEEL** MADE FROM MOTORCYCLE **TIRES.** <<<

>>> UNLIKE A **SKATEBOARD,** THESE WHIRRING ORBITWHEEL SKATES LET YOU SKATE **EVEN ON GRASS!**

# EACH year
# 50 MILLION
## red crabs
travel up to five miles (8 km) round-trip to release their **eggs.**

**WILDEBEESTS,** monarch butterflies, **JELLYFISH,** army **ANTS,** and **MANY** other **ANIMALS** also **MIGRATE** in groups of more than a **MILLION.**

## ultimate secret revealed!

### So what's up with this massive movement of crabs?

The crabs live in the rain forest on Christmas Island, located in the Indian Ocean, northwest of Australia. The journey to the coast takes about ten days. Traveling in a giant group for protection from predators, the salad-plate-size crabs scale steep cliffs and face threats from cars and yellow crazy ants. When they finally reach the beach where they were born, the females lay up to 100,000 eggs each before trekking back to their forest home.

## SKY WARS

# WHAT FLIES THE HIGHEST?

**BALD EAGLE**
**10,000** FEET
(3,000 m)

**GRAY WHALE MIGRATION**
**6,000** MILES
(9,650 km)

WINNER!

**GREEN SEA TURTLE MIGRATION**
**1,500** MILES
(2,400 km)

## ROUND & ROUND

# WHAT SPINS THE FASTEST?

**HELICOPTER BLADE**
**300** MILES AN HOUR
(483 kph)

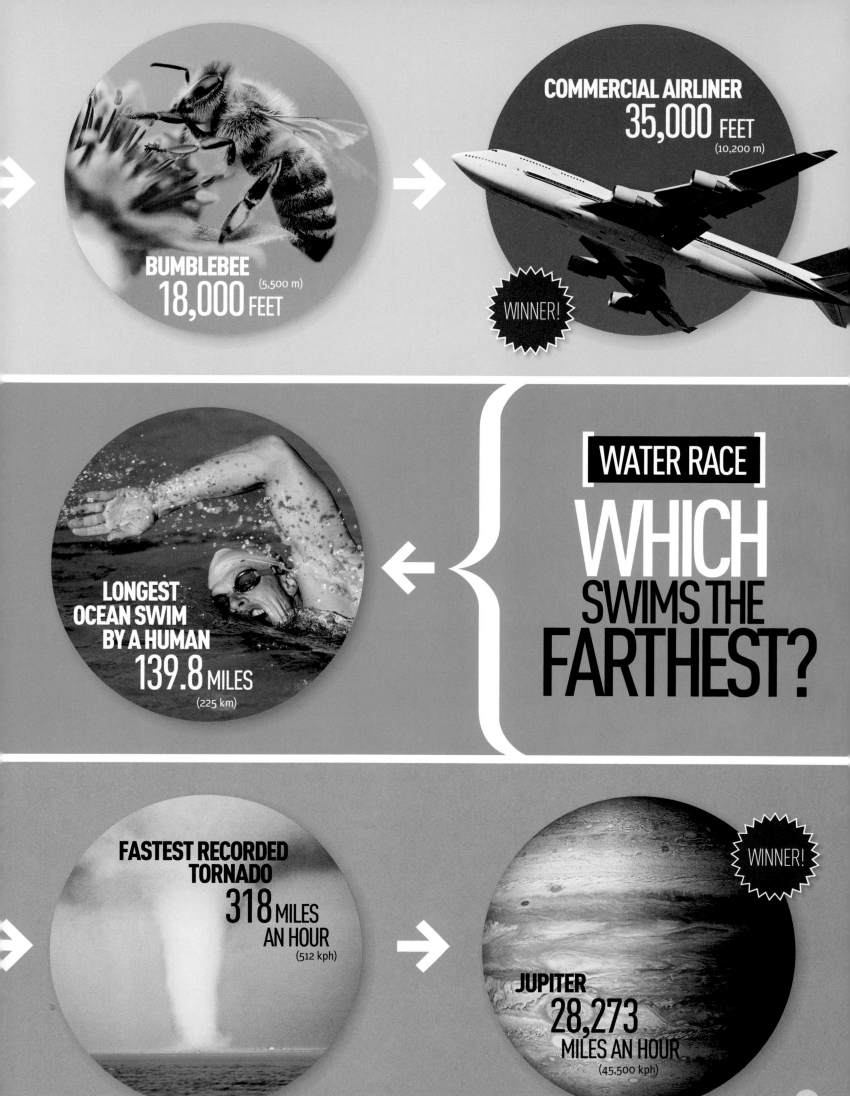

BUMBLEBEE
18,000 FEET (5,500 m)

COMMERCIAL AIRLINER
35,000 FEET (10,200 m)

WINNER!

LONGEST
OCEAN SWIM
BY A HUMAN
139.8 MILES
(225 km)

**WATER RACE**

# WHICH SWIMS THE FARTHEST?

FASTEST RECORDED TORNADO
318 MILES AN HOUR (512 kph)

JUPITER
28,273 MILES AN HOUR (45,500 kph)

WINNER!

THE **FASTEST MAN** ALIVE CAN SPRINT AS FAST AS 27 MILES AN HOUR. (43 kph)

ONE OF THE WORLD'S FASTEST SNAKES, THE **BLACK** WITH SPEEDS REACHING **150 MILES** (240 kph) **AN HOUR,** A ROLLER COASTER IN THE UNITED ARAB EMIRATES IS SO FAST RIDERS HAVE TO WEAR **SAFETY GOGGLES** TO PROTECT THEIR EYES.

A SWORDFISH CAN **SWIM** ABOUT AS FAST AS A CHEETAH CAN RUN.

**CHEETAHS** CAN ACCELERATE TO **70 MILES AN HOUR**— THAT'S AS FAST AS A CAR (112 kph) SPEEDING ON A HIGHWAY.

THE SUPERFAST ELEVATORS IN TAIWAN'S TAIPEI 101 TOWER ZOOM **84 STORIES** IN **37 SECONDS.**

**MAMBA,** SLITHERS UP TO **12** MILES AN HOUR. (19 kph)

A TRAIN IN CHINA CAN TOP **300 MILES** AN HOUR. (483 kph)

**JET.**

THE SR-71 BLACKBIRD MILITARY AIRCRAFT COULD FLY FROM NEW YORK TO LONDON IN JUST UNDER TWO HOURS—MORE THAN FOUR HOURS FASTER THAN A PASSENGER

PATAS MONKEYS CAN **SPRINT** FROM 0 TO 33 MILES AN HOUR IN JUST THREE SECONDS. (53 kph)

THE FASTEST **TENNIS SERVES** REACH SPEEDS OF MORE THAN **150 MILES AN HOUR.** (240 kph)

## Double Trouble

^ ^ ^

**NAME:**
**Mirror Image**

**WHY IT'S WILD:**
The shell of one Volkswagen is turned **upside down** on top of the other. And those legs sticking out? They belong to **inflatable dolls.**

**NAME:**
**The Glass Quilt**

**WHY IT'S WILD:**
About **10,000 marbles** and thousands of pieces of stained glass have been **glued** onto this car.

## Bugged Out!

# WiLD Rides

**NAME:**
**Pico de Gallo**

**WHY IT'S WILD:**
A salute to **Mexican mariachi** music, this car has guitars, drums, a trumpet, a saxophone, an accordion, and hundreds of **bells** attached to it.

## Auto Tune

## Cruise Control

**NAME:**
*Titanic*

**WHY IT'S WILD:**
With the **help** of some plywood and paint, this boat of a car was transformed into the *Titanic,* the famous sunken cruise ship.

## Lobsterfest

**NAME:**
**Art the Lobster**

**WHY IT'S WILD:**
This **crustacean creation** has a giant fiberglass lobster on its roof. And its tail opens like a **car trunk.**

## Road Show

**NAME:**
**Mondrian Car**

**WHY IT'S WILD:**
The owner of this art car **painted** the vehicle in the style of modern artist **Piet Mondrian,** and then made a matching roof sculpture and clothing.

## Wagon Wheels

**NAME:**
**Radio Flyer Wagon**

**WHY IT'S WILD:**
This car is a **grown-up** version of a Radio Flyer wagon and doubles as **Santa's sleigh** in the winter—complete with a fake reindeer in the front.

# In the MINUTE it takes a **sloth** to move 5 FEET...

(1.5 m)

In the same amount of time...

a human can walk **220 FEET.**
(67 m)

a cockroach can crawl **295 FEET.**
(90 m)

a greyhound can run **2,112 FEET.**
(644 m)

a horse can gallop **2,677 FEET.**
(816 m)

The British Imperial State Crown contains 2,868 diamonds, 273 pearls, 17 sapphires, 11 emeralds, and 5 rubies. It's stored with the rest of the Crown Jewels in the Tower of London. How long has this bling been there? Find out on page 116.

Britain's jewel-studded **IMPERIAL STATE CROWN** weighs more than a **FULL-GROWN** guinea pig.

CHAPTER 6

# CLAIM to FAME

Want to **spice** up your **dining** experience? These **wacky** restaurants take eating **out** to the **extreme!**

This glass-roofed **underwater** restaurant in Israel allows diners to **gaze** at fish **before** they end up on a **plate.**

**Red Sea Star**

<<<

# STRANGEST Restaurants

**Modern Toilet**

At this bathroom-themed restaurant in Taiwan, **toilets** double as **chairs** and the walls are covered with **showerheads.** Food is **served** in toilet-shaped dishes.

A team of robots provides **service** with an **electronic** smile at this Chinese eatery. The robots **move** along a white **track** that passes all of the restaurant's **21** tables.

**Dalu Robot Restaurant**

Here's a restaurant that can be **packed** up and
**shipped,** stored, or saved for a sunny day.
A Canadian company **recycles** old shipping
containers by turning them into **cafés.**

# Shipping Container Restaurant

Talk about a table with a view!
A crane in Brussels, Belgium, lifts a table
**160** feet (49 m) off the **ground** so patrons
practically dine in **midair.** Diners are
**buckled** into their seats for **safety.**

# Dinner in the Sky

Carter balances on nylon webbing that's anchored between points. The line has some bounce, like a trampoline. Tightropes, on the other hand, are pulled rigidly taut.

Carter's fancy footwork is actually known as slacklining.

Thrill seeker **Darrin Carter** balanced his way across California's Lost Arrow Spire, ~**2,890** feet (881 m) off the ground.

# Don't Look Down!

## FastFACTS

Adili Wuxor walked a tightrope strung over the Bird's Nest stadium in Beijing, China, for 5 hours a day for 60 days.

In 1974, Philippe Petit walked a tightrope wire between the World Trade Center towers. He was arrested for trespassing immediately afterward.

In 1867, Maria Spelterini became the first woman to tightrope walk across Niagara Falls. For added drama, she tried it blindfolded and then again with her feet fastened inside beach baskets.

## Party Animals

Some pets have birthday bashes that would put Hollywood stars to shame. One pup's party featured pony rides, a canine-safe cake, and a DJ spinning jams. Her birthday present: a diamond necklace!

# Furry & Fabulous!

## CHALK IT UP TO PUPPY LOVE!

LAST YEAR, U.S. PET OWNERS SPENT ABOUT **$48 BILLION** ON THEIR PETS. HERE ARE SOME OF THE MOST OUTRAGEOUS WAYS PETS HAVE BEEN **PAMPERED.**

## Clips & Curls

At pet spas, pooches can get a massage, have their nails done, or get a rainbow-colored dye job. One doggy ranch even has a bone-shaped pool!

<<<

## Designer Duds

One pet owner says her cat refuses to wear anything but a rhinestone-studded leather collar. Dogs can get in on the act with $200 cashmere sweaters and $100 raincoats.

**>>>**

## Dream Decor

Some felines live in the lap of luxury with $600 hand-carved furniture sets, such as four-poster beds and custom-built dressers. (A kitty has to have somewhere to keep her jeweled tiaras!)

## Tropical Vacations

Many hotels offer special services for four-legged guests (on their owners' bill, of course). One Mexican resort has pooch-only pool cabanas. Some hotels have room service offering doggy delights.

## Pet Estates

You'll want to be in the doghouse with these posh doggy pads. One pooch has a two-story doghouse with floor-to-ceiling windows, air-conditioning, and heated floors.

**<<<**

# 8 Frightening

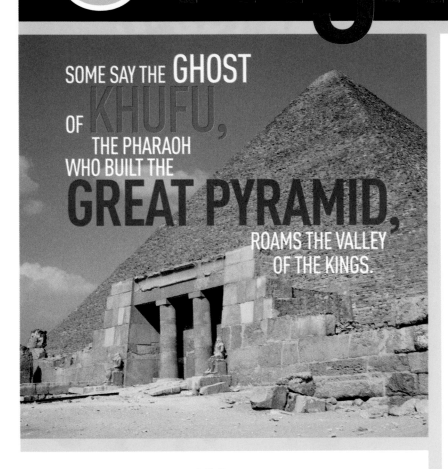

SOME SAY THE **GHOST** OF KHUFU, THE PHARAOH WHO BUILT THE **GREAT PYRAMID,** ROAMS THE VALLEY OF THE KINGS.

ACCORDING TO LEGEND **THE GHOST** OF **ABIGAIL ADAMS,** THE WIFE OF THE **2ND PRESIDENT** OF THE **UNITED STATES,** DOES **LAUNDRY** IN THE **WHITE HOUSE'S EAST ROOM.**

WHEN PARIS'S **GRAVEYARDS** BECAME OVERCROWDED, SKELETONS WERE PILED **HIGH** IN THE **CATACOMBS** DURING THE **18TH** & **19TH CENTURIES.**

## THE **SKELETONS** OF AS MANY AS **40,000** PEOPLE

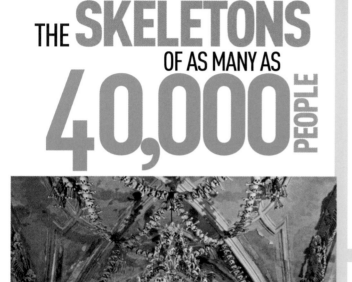

## **DECORATE** SEDLEC OSSUARY, A CHAPEL IN THE CZECH REPUBLIC.

## **BRAN CASTLE** IN ROMANIA BRIEFLY HOUSED "**VLAD DRACULA**," A 15TH-CENTURY TYRANT AND THE INSPIRATION FOR **THE MOVIE** DRACULA.

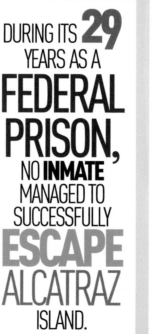

DURING ITS **29** YEARS AS A **FEDERAL PRISON**, NO **INMATE** MANAGED TO SUCCESSFULLY **ESCAPE** ALCATRAZ ISLAND.

AT THE **CATACOMBS** OF THE **CAPUCHINS** IN **SICILY**, THOUSANDS OF **MUMMIES**—FULLY CLOTHED AND ARRANGED IN POSES—**FILL ROCK-CARVED** TUNNELS.

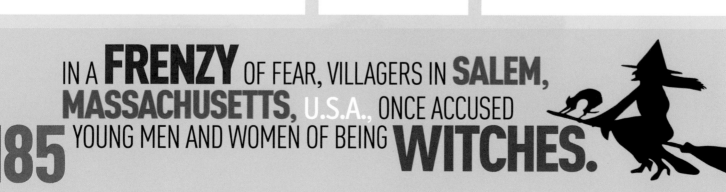

IN A **FRENZY** OF FEAR, VILLAGERS IN **SALEM, MASSACHUSETTS**, U.S.A., ONCE ACCUSED **185** YOUNG MEN AND WOMEN OF BEING **WITCHES**.

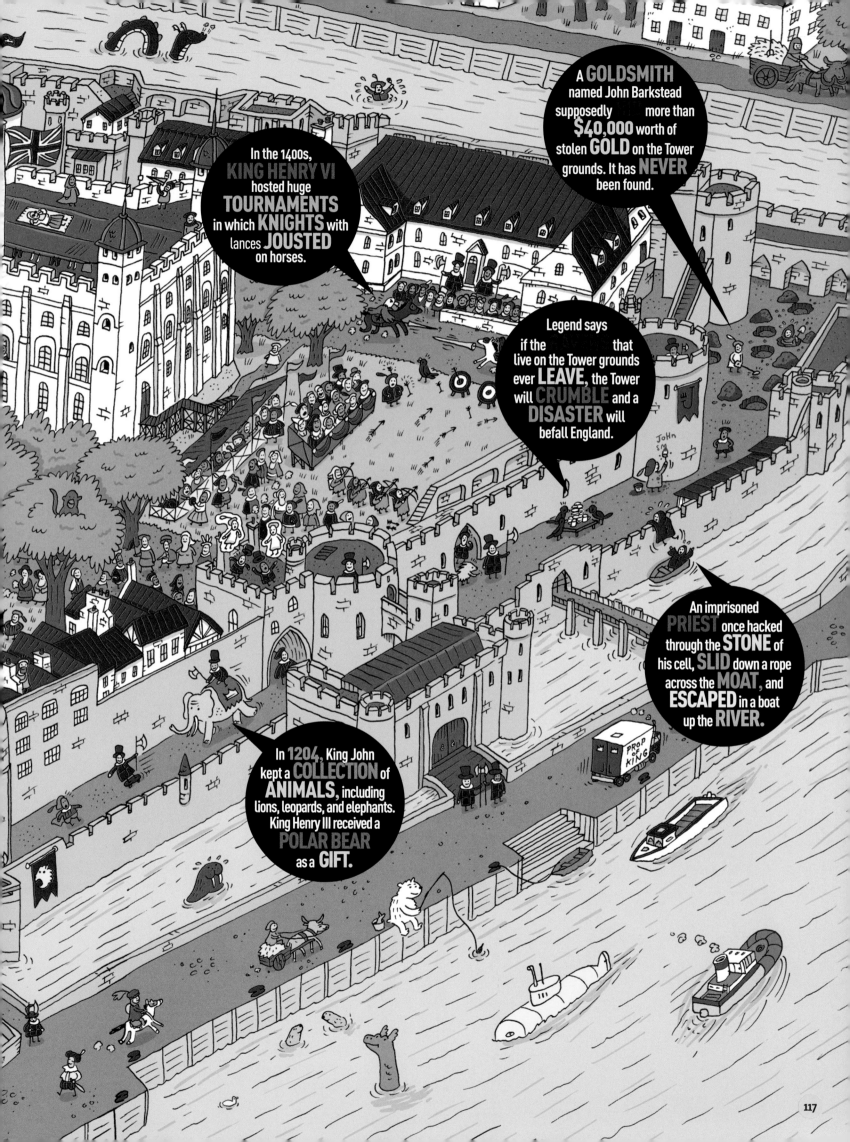

Going out of **town**? Take your **vacation** to the **extreme** with these **offbeat** accommodations.

Giraffes use their long **necks** to peek in on **guests** enjoying **breakfast** at this Kenya hotel.

<<<

## Giraffe Manor

# EXTREME Hotels

<<<

**Dog lovers** can satisfy their craze for canines at this **dog-shaped** hotel in Idaho, U.S.A. Inside a giant **wooden** beagle, you'll find a **sleeping** loft and a **reading** nook.

## Dog Bark Park Inn

In this hotel in Berlin, Germany, an eight-story aquarium contains more than 1,500 fish. Guests can see the sea life up close by taking a glass elevator through the cylindrical tank.

Fans of J. R. R. Tolkien's *Lord of the Rings* trilogy (or the recent film versions) will love this New Zealand hideaway. It's based on the fictional houses of pint-size characters called hobbits.

‹‹‹

## Hobbit Motel

## AquaDom

## Alpha Resort-Tomamu

Sleep on an ice bed and dine from ice plates at this igloo-like inn in northern Japan. All rooms, including bathrooms, are made out of ice.

At this Costa Rican rain-forest getaway, a 1965 Boeing jet has been converted to a two-bedroom suite.

## Hotel Costa Verde

›››

# Baseball Card
## MVPs

**Honus Wagner**
**SHORTSTOP / PIRATES**
Hall of Famer Honus Wagner was a shortstop in the early 1900s. Only 60 baseball cards were produced.

**HIS HOTTEST CARD:**
A card in near-perfect condition auctioned for **$2.8 million,** a record for a baseball card.

**VALUE RATING:** ★★★★★

## AMERICANS SPEND UP TO $40 MILLION ON BASEBALL CARDS EACH YEAR.

## Babe Ruth
**RIGHT OUTFIELD / YANKEES**
The "Sultan of Swat's" career home-run record stood unbroken for nearly 40 years.

**HIS HOTTEST CARD:** His 1914 Baltimore News rookie card recently fetched **$517,000**—making it the second most valuable card in the world.

**VALUE RATING:** ★★★★

## Mickey Mantle
**CENTER OUTFIELD/ YANKEES**
Baseball fans regard this Yankee slugger as one of the best switch-hitters of all time. That means he could smash home runs from both sides of the plate.

**HIS HOTTEST CARD:** His 1952 mint-condition Topps card is worth **$282,000**.

**VALUE RATING:** ★★★

## Nolan Ryan
**PITCHER / RANGERS**
A power pitcher known as the "Ryan Express," Nolan Ryan holds more strikeouts and has pitched more no-hitters than any hurler in baseball.

**HIS HOTTEST CARD:** His 1968 rookie Topps card could put **$600** in your pocket.

**VALUE RATING:** ★

## Albert Pujols
**FIRST BASE / CARDINALS**
"Prince Albert" is one of modern baseball's biggest stars. He has dominated the major hitting categories since joining the big leagues in 2001.

**HIS BIGGEST CARD:** His rookie card is valued at **$2,800**.

**VALUE RATING:** ★★

# THE WORLD-FAMOUS HOPE DIAMOND IS RUMORED TO BE CURSED!

(AND IT'S NOT THE ONLY BAUBLE WITH BAD VIBES.)

Other
treasures believed
to bring their finders
misfortune include
King Tut's tomb,
the Black Orlov diamond,
and the
Delhi Purple Sapphire.

## ultimate secret revealed!

### Can priceless treasure really be cursed? Or is this myth just a gem of a tale?

In the case of the priceless blue Hope Diamond, bad luck seemed to have plagued its series of owners for more than 300 years. After the French royal family bought the stone in 1668, tragedy struck several members of the royal court, including King Louis XVI and Marie Antoinette. They were beheaded in the French Revolution. The families of later owners were plagued with debt, mental illness, and personal disaster. Yet today, the Hope Diamond resides safely in a museum, where thousands of people a year see it—without harm!

After King Tut's treasure-filled tomb was found, one of its discoverers died. The death sparked a flurry of rumors that the boy king cursed the tomb. In reality, the stricken man was killed as a result of an infected bug bite.

KING TUT'S TOMB

# 8 Weird FACTS ABOUT

**EMPEROR JULIUS CAESAR** THREW HUGE **PARTIES** ON THE STREETS OF **ROME** WITH AS MANY AS **22,000 TABLES** PILED HIGH WITH **FOOD.**

**IVAN** THE **TERRIBLE** HAD A **SECRET POLICE** FORCE OF **6,000** BLACK-UNIFORMED GUARDS ON ALL-BLACK **HORSES.**

**EMPRESS CIXI** ROSE FROM A MIDDLE-CLASS **FAMILY** to be one of the **MOST POWERFUL WOMEN** IN THE HISTORY OF CHINA.

**GREEK** CONQUEROR

# KiNGS AND QUEENS

ACCORDING TO LEGEND,

**ATTILA THE HUN,** THE GREAT CONQUEROR, DIED OF A **NOSEBLEED** ON HIS **WEDDING NIGHT.**

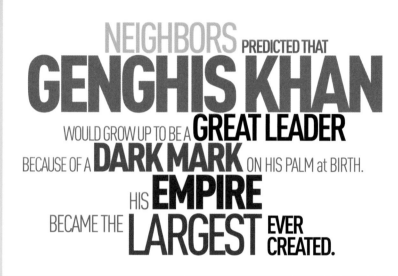

**NEIGHBORS** PREDICTED THAT **GENGHIS KHAN** WOULD GROW UP TO BE A **GREAT LEADER** BECAUSE OF A **DARK MARK** ON HIS PALM at BIRTH. HIS **EMPIRE** BECAME THE **LARGEST** EVER CREATED.

The **UNITED KINGDOM'S** CURRENT MONARCH, **QUEEN ELIZABETH,** has a royal **YOUTUBE** CHANNEL.

**MARY TUDOR,** THE FUTURE **MARY, QUEEN OF SCOTS,** WAS **CROWNED QUEEN** WHEN SHE WAS **9 MONTHS** OLD.

**ALEXANDER THE GREAT** FOUNDED AN **ASIAN CITY** IN HONOR OF HIS **FAVORITE** HORSE, BUCEPHALUS.

Mexican axolotls are endangered and live only in the wetlands of Xochimilco, Mexico. Unlike most salamanders, they stay in a tadpole-like state into adulthood, and very few ever go on dry land. What's their cutest feature? A permanent smile! Read about more strange water creatures on pages 132 and 133.

**These strange salamanders can regrow their legs and tail.**

# CHAPTER 7

# WHAT on EARTH?

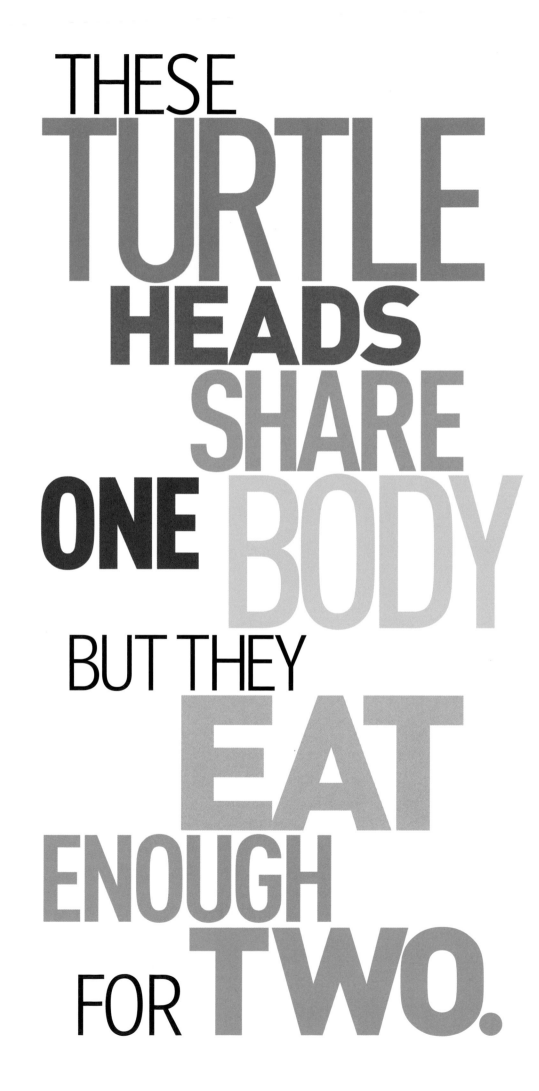

THESE **TURTLE** HEADS SHARE **ONE** BODY BUT THEY **EAT** ENOUGH FOR **TWO.**

IN **CHINA,** THIS **GOLDEN COIN SPECIES** IS CONSIDERED **GOOD LUCK.**

Get a double order!

→ Called Bracken Cave, this bat **hideout** is located near San Antonio, Texas, U.S.A.

→ It can take more than **three hours** for all of the bats to **exit** the cave.

→ The bats fly out every summer evening to feed, then return at **dawn.**

→ The **giant cloud** of bats shows up on the radar at a nearby airport.

→ Inside the cave, as many as **500 baby** bats squeeze into one square foot (30.5 cubic cm) **to stay warm.**

# 20 MILLION BATS

## LIVE in the WORLD'S LARGEST bat colony!

### Deep-Sea Anglerfish >>>

**WHERE IT LIVES:**
**Eastern and Northern Atlantic Ocean**

**WHY IT'S STRANGE:**
This freaky-looking fish lives so deep in the ocean that it swims in complete **darkness**. A "fishing rod" juts out of its **forehead** with a lure at the end that is **luminous** to attract prey.

# Strangest FiSH in the Sea

Eyes

Nares
(Nostrils)

Mouth

### Barreleye Fish

**WHERE IT LIVES:**
**Pacific Ocean**

**WHY IT'S STRANGE:**
Its head is **see-through!** The fish's eyes **swivel** up and down, so it can look through its own head to **scope** out prey.

**WHERE IT LIVES:**
**North Pacific**

**WHY IT'S STRANGE:**
This **slinky** sea creature got its name because it **slithers** through the water like an eel, but it's actually a fish.

### Wolf Eel

# Leafy Sea Dragon

**WHERE IT LIVES:**
off the coast of Australia

**WHY IT'S STRANGE:**
The leafy sea dragon's plantlike look **camouflages** the fish in seaweed, where it can **hide** from predators.

**WHERE IT LIVES:**
worldwide in deep coastal waters

**WHY IT'S STRANGE:**
The shark's **bizarre beak** helps it sense prey. Then it **impales** its catch with those fang-like **teeth**.

# Rosy-Lipped Batfish

**WHERE IT LIVES:**
tropical Western Atlantic Ocean

**WHY IT'S STRANGE:**
This "glamorous" fish looks like it's wearing **lipstick**, but that's not really makeup. The bright color may help members of the species **recognize** each other.

# Goblin Shark

**WHERE IT LIVES:**
New Zealand coast

**WHY IT'S STRANGE:**
Officially called a **fathead** sculpin fish, this species was only recently discovered. The fish became an instant Internet sensation and even has a **Facebook** page.

# Blobfish

This isn't really a nose; it's a flap of flabby skin.

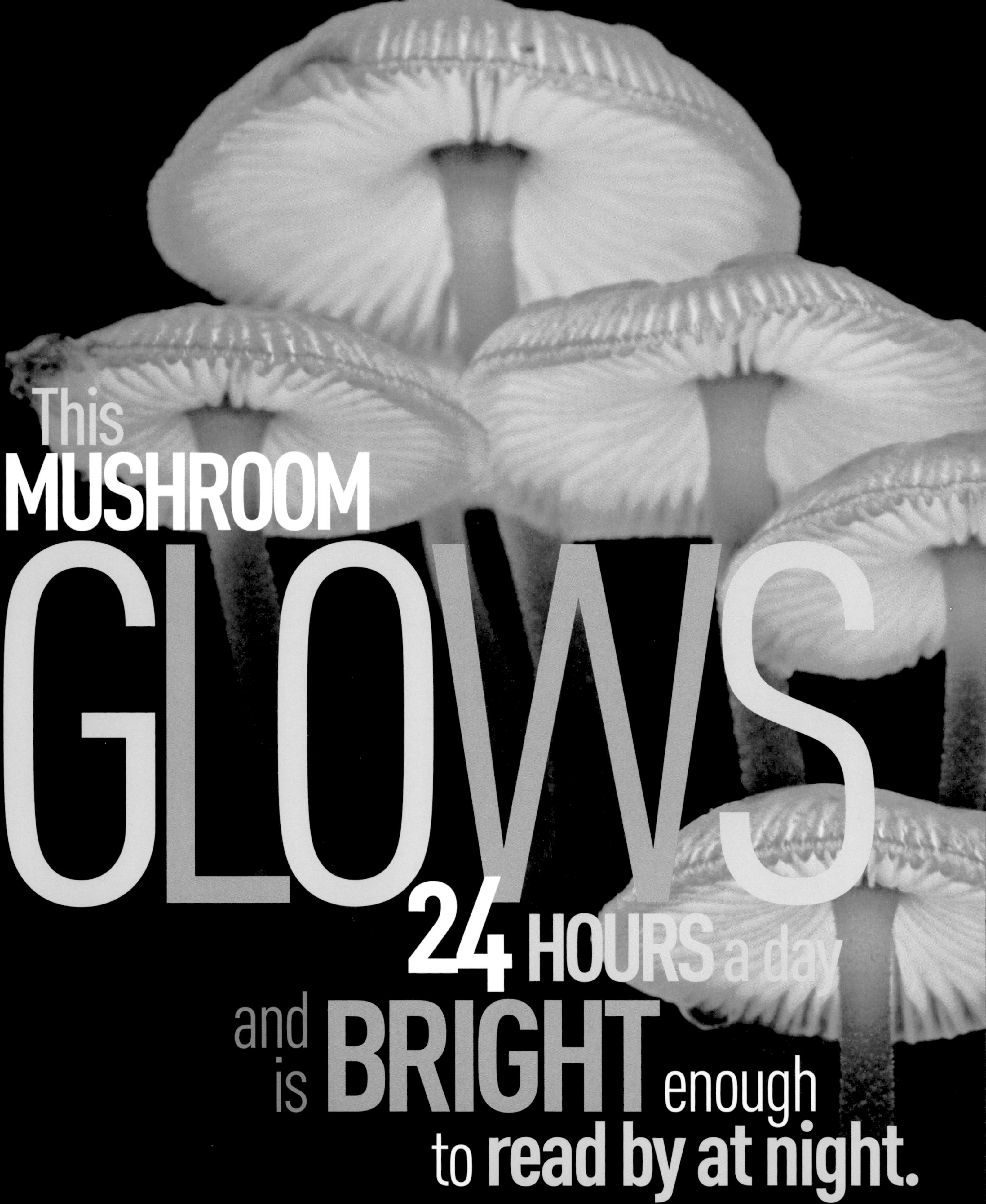

This
**MUSHROOM**
**GLOWS**
**24** **HOURS** a day
and **BRIGHT** enough
is **to read by at night.**

# Fireflies, glow worms, click beetles, railroad worms, Malaysian land snails, fire centipedes, and other animals also glow

## ultimate secret revealed!

**How do these mushrooms and animals turn on the light without flipping a switch?** They are bioluminescent, which means they generate "cold light," or light that does not create heat. This natural glow is created when two natural chemicals, luciferin and luciferase, are combined within living things. Now that's an *illuminating* fact!

# FROM SECRETS CARVED IN STONE

TO HIDDEN MESSAGES SCRATCHED INTO THE EARTH, THE DISCOVERY OF SOME OF HISTORY'S MOST INTRIGUING MYSTERIES LEADS TO MORE QUESTIONS THAN ANSWERS.

# EARTH'S Greatest Mysteries

## Stonehenge

(Wiltshire, England, U.K.) About 4,500 years ago, people began creating this mysterious circle of stones. No one knows exactly how or why these ancient people transported the enormous stones, some as heavy as ten large African elephants, to this site.

<<<

## Great Sphinx >>> of Giza

(Giza, Egypt) For thousands of years no one knew who built the massive Sphinx statue near Egypt's two largest pyramids. Recent archaeological excavations found that it may be a self-portrait of Pharaoh Khafre—who built one of the pyramids—in the shape of the Egyptian god Horus.

# Nasca Lines

(Nasca, Peru) Alien landing strips? Mystical calendars? These are some of the far-fetched explanations for the 2,000-year-old giant drawings—best viewed from the air—of animals, people, and shapes etched into the plains. No one knows for sure, but the ancient Nasca people may have created the drawings to pray for rain.

# Machu Picchu

(Near Cusco, Peru) The mountaintop city of Machu Picchu, built around 1460, was home to some 700 Inca, a group of South American Indians, until the people suddenly fled. Experts suspect the city was a sacred place, but exactly why it was built and then abandoned remains a mystery.

# Terra Cotta Warriors

(near Xi'an, China) When archaeologists unearthed a pit filled with thousands of life-size clay soldiers and other artifacts in 1974, they knew this was the work of China's first emperor, Qin Shi Huang Di. But they didn't know *why* he built this clay army 2,200 years ago. One possibility? Protection from his enemies' ghosts in the afterlife.

# Moai Statues

(Easter Island, South Pacific) When Europeans discovered Easter Island in 1722, they found giant stone heads, now called moai statues. But where did the carvers of these 887 statues go? No people lived on the remote island, 2,300 miles (3,700 km) off the coast of South America. To this day, no one knows what happened to them.

137

## FastFACTS

**NAME:** Cave of Crystals
**LOCATION:** Near Chihuahua, Mexico
**DEPTH:** Almost 1,000 feet (300 m)
**DISCOVERED:** In 2000

# CRYSTAL CAVES

## CrystalCREATIONS

This underground crystal palace formed over hundreds of thousands of years. Groundwater mixed with minerals trickled through the cave and was heated by magma, or molten rock, from below Earth's surface. When the mixture cooled to about 136°F (58°C), the minerals began converting to selenite, which slowly formed the gigantic crystals.

**THE LARGEST CRYSTALS ARE ABOUT 600,000 YEARS OLD.**

# This **cave** contains the **WORLD'S LARGEST** known natural **crystals**— one is as **LONG** as a **school bus!**

THESE EXPLORERS ARE WEARING SPECIAL COOLING SUITS SO THEY DON'T GET OVERHEATED.

SOME OF THE CRYSTAL BEAMS WEIGH AS MUCH AS 24 TONS (22 T)— THAT'S MORE THAN 3 AFRICAN ELEPHANTS.

A FINGERNAIL CAN EASILY SCRATCH THESE DELICATE CRYSTALS, WHICH ARE MADE OF A NATURAL SUBSTANCE CALLED SELENITE.

THE TEMPERATURE INSIDE THE CAVE IS A STEAMY 136°F (58°C).

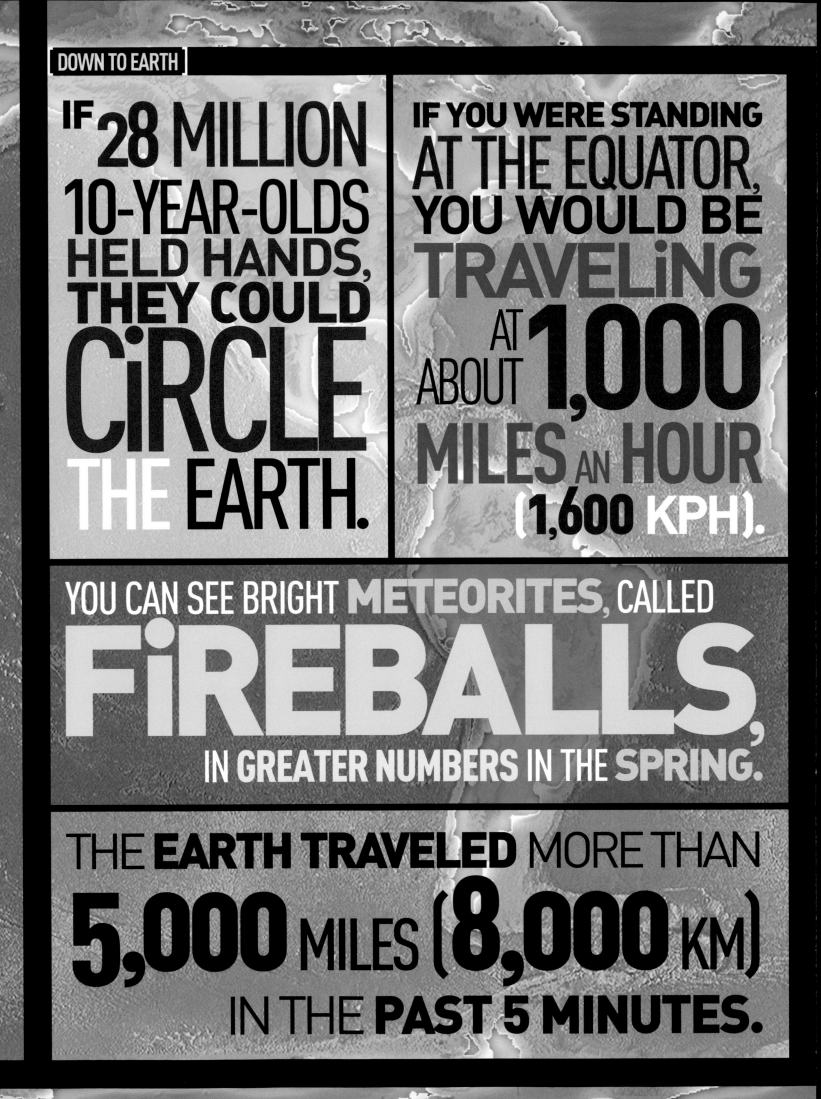

IF 28 MILLION 10-YEAR-OLDS HELD HANDS, THEY COULD CIRCLE THE EARTH.

IF YOU WERE STANDING AT THE EQUATOR, YOU WOULD BE TRAVELING AT ABOUT 1,000 MILES AN HOUR (1,600 KPH).

YOU CAN SEE BRIGHT METEORITES, CALLED FIREBALLS, IN GREATER NUMBERS IN THE SPRING.

THE EARTH TRAVELED MORE THAN 5,000 MILES (8,000 KM) IN THE PAST 5 MINUTES.

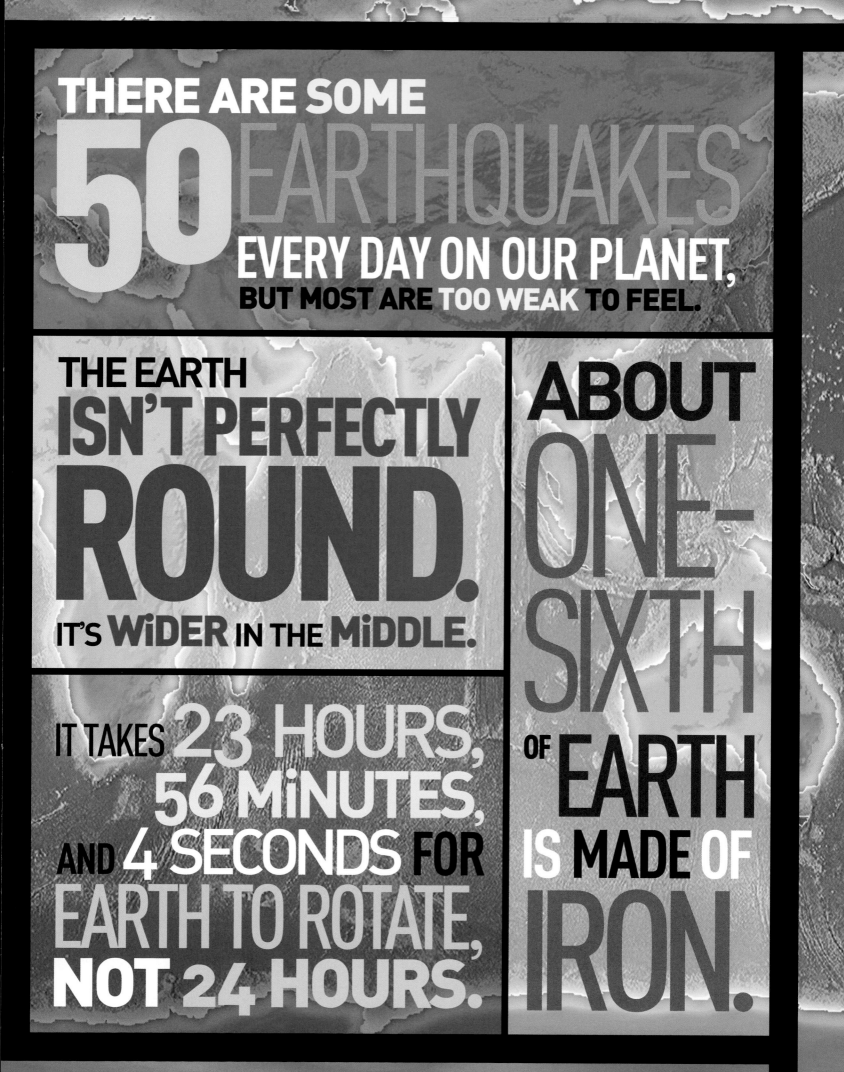

THERE ARE SOME **50** EARTHQUAKES EVERY DAY ON OUR PLANET, BUT MOST ARE TOO WEAK TO FEEL.

THE EARTH ISN'T PERFECTLY **ROUND.** IT'S **WiDER** IN THE **MiDDLE.**

IT TAKES **23** HOURS, **56** MiNUTES, AND **4** SECONDS FOR EARTH TO ROTATE, **NOT 24** HOURS.

ABOUT **ONE-SIXTH** OF EARTH IS MADE OF IRON.

THE STUNNING STRIPES WERE EXPOSED WHEN THE OUTER ICE MELTED AWAY.

MOST ICEBERGS ARE WHITE, BUT SOME ARE GREEN OR BLUE.

AN ICEBERG IS A GIANT CHUNK OF ICE THAT BREAKS OFF OF A GLACIER OR ICE SHEET.

ICEBERGS CAN BE MORE THAN 5,000 YEARS OLD.

# BLUE STRIPES CAN FORM IN ICEBERGS WHEN WATER FILLS CRACKS IN THE ICE AND THEN FREEZES.

# LONG-LOST RELATIVES

Check out these totally *wild* cousins!

## CHICKEN AND *T. REX*

**WHAT'S THE CONNECTION?**
Comparisons recently confirmed chickens and *T. Rex* share similar collagen proteins—components of the strong fibers in tissues such as tendons, ligaments, and cartilage. That's a strong sign they share the same genetic makeup.

**FAMILY SECRETS:** Shake a dinosaur's family tree and a bird falls out! Modern birds, such as chickens, are the living descendants of dinosaurs, such as the *Tyrannosaurus rex!*

## PIG AND CAMEL

**WHAT'S THE CONNECTION?**
These two share a rabbit-size ancestor that lived 50 to 55 million years ago.

**FAMILY SECRETS:** To see the family resemblance, look at their toes. Pigs and camels both come from a long family line with an even number of toes on each foot. Also in the family? Cows and hippos.

# WHALE, DOLPHIN, AND HIPPOPOTAMUS

**WHAT'S THE CONNECTION?**
They are all related to a four-footed and hoofed mammal that lived 50 to 60 million years ago.

**FAMILY SECRETS:** Over time, the family split. Whales (dolphins are part of the whale family) lost their hooves and stayed in the sea, while hippos became amphibious animals that now live in water and on land.

# MANATEE AND ELEPHANT

**WHAT'S THE CONNECTION?**
They have a common relative that was about the size of a small dog and lived more than 60 million years ago.

**FAMILY SECRETS:** Though elephants and manatees don't look like long-lost twins, the structure of their hearts and the arrangement of their teeth are similar.

A *T.REX* could probably eat up to **500 pounds** of meat in (227 kg) **one bite.**

You can spot this fierce *T. rex* statue in a museum in Drumheller, Alberta, Canada. What else attracts dino-loving road trippers to the town? Find out on page 164.

# CHAPTER 8

WiLD&
WACkY

## Giant Cupcake

**WHY IT'S FREAKY:**
It took **24 hours** and 240 pounds (109 kg) of eggs to bake this **four-and-a-half foot** (1.4-m)-tall cupcake, which weighs more than two motorcycles!

# FREAKY FOODS

## The Big Cheese

**WHY IT'S FREAKY:**
A sculptor spent **40 hours** carving Abraham Lincoln out of a **1,000-pound** (454-kg) block of cheddar cheese.

## Scorpions On Sticks

**WHY IT'S FREAKY:**
Though they may seem freaky to some, these **skewered** scorpions—deep-fried and sprinkled with spices—are considered a **delicacy** in China.

## Bite-size Fast Food

**WHY IT'S FREAKY:**
Hope you're **not hungry.** The cheeseburger in this mini-meal is only an **inch** (2.5 cm) wide!

## Square Watermelon

›››

**WHY IT'S FREAKY:**
The melons, grown inside a **cube-shaped** glass box to get their square shape, cost about **$75 each.**

## Jell-O Architecture

‹‹‹

**WHY IT'S FREAKY:**
To create this **wiggly** replica of the Palace of Fine Arts in San Francisco, California, an artist filled special **rubber molds** with different colors of Jell-O. Each sculpture took a few **months** to complete.

**WHY IT'S FREAKY:**
At more than **200 pounds** (91 kg), this cake is a complete replica of a giant octopus, right down to the **tentacles** and suckers.

## Octopus Cake

# PEANUT BUTTER
## can be converted into a

Anything that's made of carbon can be turned into a diamond. And every plant and animal on Earth is made up of some carbon. One recipe?

1. Squeeze peanut butter between two diamonds.

2. Expose to extremely high pressure at 3,632°F (2,000°C).

3. Take cover in case of explosion.

4. The catch? Only highly trained scientists in a special laboratory have ever done this.

# DIAMOND.

So can
broccoli, flower petals,
butterfly wings,
& pencils

(and most natural things on Earth).

# StreetWise

**COOL FACTS** ARE HANGING OUT AROUND EVERY CORNER OF THIS **NEIGHBORHOOD.** TAKE A TOUR TO IMPROVE YOUR STREET SMARTS.

Some **CARS** can run on used **FRENCH-FRY** oil.

A **DOG** can make about **100** different facial **EXPRESSIONS.**

Some **FISH** can **WALK** on **LAND!**

The **ODDS** that an average **GOLFER** will make a **HOLE IN ONE** during a game are **12,000 to 1.**

**POPSICLES** were **INVENTED** by an **11-YEAR-OLD.**

# Festival FuN

ON INTERNATIONAL **PILLOW FIGHT DAY—** USUALLY IN MARCH OR APRIL— PEOPLE IN MORE THAN **130 CITIES** HOLD GIANT OUTDOOR PILLOW FIGHTS.

AT THE **LEMON FESTIVAL** IN MENTON, FRANCE, AN ARTIST MADE THIS REPLICA OF **EGYPT'S** GREAT **SPHINX STATUE** FROM **ORANGES** AND **LEMONS.**

YOU'LL SEE **DOUBLE** WHEN THOUSANDS OF TWINS GATHER AT THE **TWINS DAYS FEST,** HELD IN — WHERE ELSE?— TWINSBURG, OHIO, U.S.A.

AT THE **MONKEY FESTIVAL** IN LOP BURI, THAILAND, TOWNSPEOPLE SEEKING **GOOD FORTUNE** HONOR **MONKEYS** WITH FRESH FLOWERS AND FEASTS OF FRUIT, VEGGIES, AND SWEETS.

EACH **HALLOWEEN,** DOZENS OF DOGS DRESS UP IN THEIR **CUTEST COSTUMES** FOR A **PET PARADE** IN NEW YORK CITY, NEW YORK, U.S.A.

REVELERS AT **LA TOMATINA FESTIVAL** IN SPAIN **SLING** 100 TONS OF TOMATOES AT (90 t) EACH OTHER IN THE WORLD'S BIGGEST **FOOD FIGHT!**

# 8 Amazing FEATS BY

A woman in India **danced** for 123 hours and 15 minutes without stopping.

AN AMERICAN MAN USED **10,000** TOOTHPICKS TO BUILD A FOUR-FOOT-LONG (1.2 m) REMOTE-CONTROL BOAT.

A MAN WALKED ON HIS HANDS FROM VIENNA, AUSTRIA, TO PARIS, FRANCE. THE TRIP TOOK **55** DAYS!

AN ARTIST IN OHIO USED **26,666 bars of soap** to sculpt a MASSIVE WINGED PIG named Sudsie.

# WILD & WACKY

A **SKYDIVER** in Indiana, U.S.A., **parachuted** out of an airplane **640** times in **24 hours.**

A MAN IN THE U.K. **GREW** A **GIANT ZUCCHINI** THAT WEIGHED AS MUCH AS A LARGE SHEEPDOG.

A SCULPTOR **created** a statue of **HIMSELF** using his own **HAIR, TEETH,** and **NAILS.**

A NEW ZEALAND WOMAN **RAN** **100 METERS** (328 FT) IN **18.5 SECONDS** WEARING **FLIPPERS ON HER FEET.**

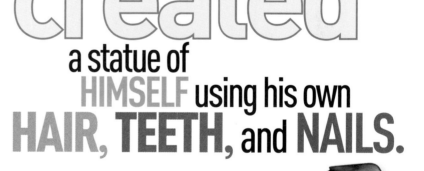

PEOPLE WHO **COLLECT** PEZ DISPENSERS ARE CALLED **"PEZHEADS."**

THE WORLD'S **LARGEST** PEZ - DISPENSING MACHINE STANDS 7 FEET, 10 INCHES (2.4 M) TALL AND HAS A **SNOWMAN HEAD.**

**STAR WARS** FIGURES ARE THE MOST POPULAR **MOVIE-CHARACTER** PEZ DISPENSERS.

AMERICANS EAT MORE THAN **THREE BILLION** PEZ CANDIES **EVERY YEAR.**

PEZ CANDY COMES IN **TEN FLAVORS,** SUCH AS CHERRY, CHOCOLATE, **COLA,** AND SOUR WATERMELON.

ONE MAN OWNS **5,000** PEZ DISPENSERS— ONE OF THE **WORLD'S LARGEST** COLLECTIONS OF THE PRODUCT.

A museum in CALIFORNIA, U.S.A., DISPLAYS MORE THAN 900 PEZ dispensers—ONE OF EVERY DESIGN EVER SOLD.

THE NAME **PEZ** IS A SHORTENED VERSION OF THE GERMAN WORD FOR PEPPERMINT, *PFEFFERMINZ.*

# Silly Styles

THIS **SKIRT** DOUBLES AS A **VENDING MACHINE** DISGUISE WHEN YOU WANT TO **GO** UNDERCOVER. >>>

THIS ECO-FRIENDLY **BAG** IS MADE FROM >> **365** RECYCLED **COMPUTER KEYBOARD KEYS.**

A SPANISH DESIGNER >>> GLUED TOGETHER MORE THAN **200** COLORFUL **PLASTIC BALLS** TO CREATE THIS "**BALL GOWN.**"

THESE **WEDDING GOWNS** ARE MADE OF **TOILET PAPER.** THEY COULD BE HANDY HANKIES IF THE BRIDE GETS **CHOKED UP.** ⌄ ⌄ ⌄

^ ^ ^ EVER GET SO **HUNGRY** YOU COULD EAT YOUR SHOES? **THESE "LOAFERS"** ARE MADE FROM **REAL BREAD** AND COME IN **WHITE AND WHOLE WHEAT.**

THIS HEADPIECE, MADE FROM **CRUSHED AND CUT SODA CANS** AND **WIRE, IS HARD TO TOP!** ⌄ ⌄ ⌄

**THE ARTIST** WHO MADE THESE ^ ^ ^ **AP-*PEAL*-ING SHOES** CONSIDERS THEM **WEARABLE** SCULPTURES.

# GREAT WhiTE Gator!

Anyone have sunscreen?

BOUYA BLAN IS NOT ALBINO. ALBINO ANIMALS HAVE RED OR PINK EYES; BOUYA'S EYES ARE BLUE.

THIS RARE REPTILE PROBABLY WOULDN'T SURVIVE IN THE WILD BECAUSE IT LACKS NATURAL CAMOUFLAGE TO HELP IT HIDE FROM PREDATORS.

BOUYA BLAN IS ONE OF 19 WHITE ALLIGATORS COLLECTED AS HATCHLINGS FROM A NEW ORLEANS, LOUISIANA, U.S.A., SWAMP. ONLY A FEW SURVIVED.

WHITE GATORS CAN GET SUNBURNED.

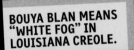
BOUYA BLAN MEANS "WHITE FOG" IN LOUISIANA CREOLE.

There are **only** **15** known WHITE ALLIGATORS in the world.

## >>> Peachoid Water Tower

**WHERE:**
Gaffney,
South Carolina, U.S.A.

**WHY IT'S ZANY:**
It took **50 gallons** (189 L) of paint in 20 colors to get the perfect **peach** shade for this four-story water tower.

## Dinosaur Capital of the World

**WHERE:**
**Drumheller, Alberta, Canada**

**WHY IT'S ZANY:**
This town is dizzy with dinos! Its land is rich in fossils, and prehistoric animals greet you wherever you go, from an 82-foot (25-m)-tall roadside dinosaur statue to the *T. rex* statue (above) at the town's paleontology museum.

# ZanY ROAD TRiP!

## The Leaning Tower of Niles

**WHERE: Niles, Illinois, U.S.A.**

**WHY IT'S ZANY:**
Built in honor of scientist Galileo Galilei, this **water tower** looks—and leans—just like the real deal in Italy, only it's **half** the size!

<<<

# Signpost Forest

**WHERE:**
Watson Lake, Yukon, Canada

**WHY IT'S ZANY:**
What started with **one sign** tacked to a post in 1942 has grown to a collection of **64,000 signs** today.

<<<

# Fremont Troll

**WHERE:**
Seattle, Washington, U.S.A.

**WHY IT'S ZANY:**
Litterbugs, **beware!** This 18-foot (5.5-m)-tall troll's "job" is to stop people from **dumping trash** under a bridge.

<<<

# Big Gumboot

**WHERE:**
Tully, Queensland, Australia

**WHY IT'S ZANY:**
The town of Tully built this 26-foot (8-m)-high **rain boot** to celebrate its title as the **wettest** place in Australia. The green tree frog is a nod to Tully's abundant amphibians, which thrive in the wet weather.

# Cadillac Ranch

**WHERE:**
Amarillo, Texas, U.S.A.

**WHY IT'S ZANY:**
These spray-painted Cadillacs are stuck **hood-first** in a pasture.

This **LIFE-SIZE** transformer was made of parts from **100** of London's double-decker **BUSES.**

Oxford Circus
25

Buy your ticket before boarding

ticket before boa

More than 60,000 Twitter users voted for the creation of the 13-foot (4-m) Transformer—called Bendy-Bus Prime—to celebrate the DVD release of a Transformers film. Check out another mind-boggling bot on page 182.

166

# CHAPTER 9

# INTELLIGENT LIFE

# 8 ANIMAL GENIUSES

AN **ORCHESTRA** OF **16 ELEPHANTS** IN **THAILAND** CRANKS OUT **TUNES** ON **JUMBO-SIZE** XYLOPHONES, DRUMS, & CHIMES.

NORA, A **PIANO-PLAYING** TABBY, BEGAN MAKING **"MUSIC"** AFTER HOPPING ON A **PIANO BENCH** AND PUTTING HER **PAWS** TO THE KEYS.

TALK ABOUT FORTUNE-TELLING **TENTACLES!** AN **OCTOPUS** NAMED **PAUL** CORRECTLY PREDICTED THE **EIGHT** OUTCOMES OF **2010 WORLD CUP** MATCHES.

# in ACTION

BY ITS FIRST BIRTHDAY, A DOLPHIN CHOOSES A "SIGNATURE WHISTLE" THAT FUNCTIONS AS ITS NAME.

MANY ZOO ANIMALS "PAINT" TO WARD OFF BOREDOM, BUT A BONOBO NAMED KANZI ACTUALLY NAMES HIS PAINTINGS AS A HUMAN ARTIST WOULD.

CROWS FORM HOOKS OUT OF LEAF STEMS TO FISH GRUBS FROM HARD-TO-REACH PLACES.

MARGAYS, WILD CATS OF THE AMAZON, IMITATE THE CALLS OF MONKEYS TO DRAW THEM NEAR FOR A SNACK.

WHEN HONEYBEES NEED A NEW BEEHIVE, BEE "SCOUTS" COMMUNICATE NEW ADDRESS OPTIONS WITH DANCES. THEIR HIVE MATES VOTE ON A WINNER.

High-tech **POLICE STATIONS** will soar through the **SKIES** like airborne **cruise SHIPS.**

One day, flying **DRONES** will deliver **PACKAGES** and **PIZZAS.**

Aquarium

Spaceport

Science Museum

Cities will **CREATE** lanes for speedy **PERSONAL** transportation vehicles such as **MOTORIZED CHAIRS** and hoverboards.

Your **CLOSET** will contain just **ONE** all-purpose **OUTFIT** that can **CHANGE** shape and color depending on what you feel like **WEARING** that day.

# FutureWorld

## FAR-OUT THINGS YOU CAN LOOK FORWARD TO!

**CLONING** technology could bring **EXTINCT ANIMALS** back to life.

**HUMANS** will call on **ROBOTS** to handle ROUTINE CHORES like walking the **DOG**.

**POLICE** will use **HI-TECH** "truth-sensing" **GLASSES** to help them know if a **SUSPECT** was involved in a **CRIME**.

These **six** amazing **gizmos** could ride the **wave** of the **future.**

# COOL Inventions

## Jetting Around

>>>

**Blast off** with a **jetpack** that sends its wearer **aloft** with **two** powerful fans. **Controls** on the jetpack's arms allow the pilot to adjust **speed** and **direction**, and an **emergency** parachute is included (**just in case!**).

This sleek, seamless **airplane** is a promising design for **Earth-friendly** flights. The lightweight, **aerodynamic** design of this blended-wing plane could **cut** fuel use in **half.**

## Green Air Travel

## Brain Games

>>>

By **measuring** brain activity, a device called **MindSet** allows you to **control** video games with your **thoughts.**

Certain **materials** can **convert** electricity into **sound.** Using these materials, scientists have invented a **paper-thin** film that may be able to turn any wall into a **speaker.**

## Singing Wallpaper
**‹‹‹**

A **bionic** contact lens contains electronic **circuits** that are one-thousandth the width of a **human hair.** **Future** versions could feature a **display** that **projects** images into your **eyes** that only you can see.

**ˇ**
**ˇ**
**ˇ**

## Exosuits
**‹‹‹**

**Robotic** outfits called XOS exoskeletons will give **soldiers** of the future **superhuman** strength.

## Super-powered Sight

# GREENING the RED PLANET

One day humans might live on Mars. Here's how it could become the new Earth in 1,000 years.

### YEAR ZERO
The project might begin with a series of missions to set up living quarters.

### YEAR 100
Human-built factories that spew potent greenhouse gases work to boost Mars's atmosphere. The global warming that results from the greenhouse gas buildup will thaw the frozen planet.

### YEAR 200
Rain would fall and water would flow once enough carbon dioxide had been released. Microbes, algae, and lichens could start growing on rocks.

Living in space can cause some weird side effects. By monitoring astronauts on shuttle flights and on the International Space Station, researchers have been studying the effects that being away from Earth can have on the body. Here are a few out-of-this-world observations.

**NEW HEIGHTS:** Decreased pressure on the spine causes most space travelers to grow two or more inches (5+ cm).

**QUEASY FEELING:** Nearly every astronaut experiences space sickness, which includes nausea and headaches.

**SLEEPY SILENCE:** Astronauts who snored on Earth have been found to sleep silently in space.

**PASS THE TISSUES:** A weightless environment causes the body's fluids to shift upward, resulting in nasal congestion and facial puffiness.

**GRAVITY AGAIN:** Some space station veterans say that the hardest thing to get used to after returning to Earth is gravity—when an object is released in midair and falls.

## YEAR 600

Microbes would create organic soil and add oxygen to the atmosphere. Introduced flowering plants and evergreen forests might take root.

## YEAR 1,000

Since oxygen levels would remain low, humans on Mars would require scuba gear to breathe outside. Energy for cities might come from nuclear power and wind turbines.

## Doggone Funny

To rob a grocery store, a thief attempted to disguise himself by wearing a mask that looked like Pluto, the cartoon dog. But the clerk took one look at the goofy disguise and burst out laughing. The humiliated bad guy fled the scene—without any cash.

>>>

# Stupid Criminals BUSTED!

## FORGET THE PERFECT CRIME!

THESE BUNGLING BURGLARS WERE PRACTICALLY BEGGING TO BE CAUGHT. HERE ARE **SIX** FAILED CRIME ATTEMPTS THAT ARE POSITIVELY **CRIMINAL**.

<<<

## Dumpster Diving

When a thief wriggled underneath a Dumpster to steal some valuable copper wiring, he wasn't planning on spending time there. But after squeezing underneath, the robber got stuck and couldn't get out! He spent the whole night there. The copper caper mastermind was probably grateful to see the police—who rescued him—even though it meant being arrested.

## Steal & Snooze

After a department store break-in, police officers followed a trail of stolen items. The trail led to a field near the store's parking lot. There, the officers found two thieves fast asleep. One rested his head on a stolen chair cushion; the other snuggled on a swiped hammock. The thieves learned a hard lesson: Don't fall asleep on the job.

## All Wet

A business owner thought he was being robbed—until he saw the thief's "gun" dripping water. The thief was armed with a water pistol! When the owner realized that he wasn't in any danger, he refused to hand over any cash. The thief ran away with the police hot on his trail.

## Tight Squeeze

A would-be robber tried to squeeze through a shop window—the problem was, the window was no bigger than this book and the robber got stuck! After hearing his cries for help, the shop owner called the police to pull the trapped thief out.

## Slow-Speed Chase

You've heard of a getaway car. But a getaway lawn mower? That's exactly what one criminal tried to use to escape the scene of a crime. After trashing a building, a vandal puttered away on a riding lawn mower. Police busted the gardening gangster when a cruiser blocked the mower's path.

→ Marvey calls this stunt **the Ultimate Cut.**

→ An **illusion** is something that appears to be different from the way it is in reality.

→ The **sawing** trick has been performed at magic shows for nearly **100 years.**

Magician **Peter Marvey's** bottom half appears to ride a unicycle around the stage, while his **top half** stays put!

# MiND

→ This **trick** is a variation of a popular illusion where a volunteer enters a box that the magician appears to **saw** in half.

King **penguin** Nils Olav is an **honorary** colonel-in-chief in the **Norwegian** King's Guard.

**Ten Hut!**

**Venomous** scorpions keep precious **jewels** safe from **shifty** fingers at a Michigan, U.S.A., **jewelry** store.

>>>

**Stinging Security**

# ANiMALS
## Acting Like Us!

Maybe **animals** aren't so **different** from **humans** after all . . .

>>>

When **stressed-out** chickens lost their **plumage**, a United Kingdom woman had jumpers (sweaters) **knitted** for the **balding** birds.

**Best-Dressed Hens**

## Camera Ham

Photographer **Paul Nicklen** made an **unexpected** best friend while snapping **pictures** of **leopard seals in Antarctica.** This seal brought Nicklen **"gifts"** of **penguins.**

<<<

## Baby Doll Love

<<<

Young **female** chimps **play** with sticks and logs as if they're **infants,** probably as **practice** for motherhood.

## Love Your Cologne >>>

Cats dig cool scents just like people do. Zookeepers in the U.S.A. **spray** men's **cologne** around the cats' **enclosures** to exercise their noses.

The head contains two cameras housed within Robovie's large, round eyes. Motors within the camera generate humanlike eye movements.

Two microphones pick up human voices.

That lettuce looks tasty! The salad dressing is in aisle 5.

ROBOVIE

ATR

This **ROBOT** NAMED **ROBOVIE** helps you shop for groceries!

Three wheels keep Robovie on a roll while roaming the supermarket aisles.

# SHOPbot

Hinged arms are equipped with touch sensors so they can detect and carry shopping baskets.

From home, shoppers upload their shopping lists to a store's Robovie through a mobile phone app. When shoppers arrive at the store, Robovie is waiting to greet them.

## FastFACTS

### ROBOVIE BY THE NUMBERS

Stands 4 feet (1.2 m) tall

Weighs 88 pounds (40 kg)

Operates for 4 hours before needing a recharge

Includes 24 ultrasonic sensors for navigating around obstacles

### BOTS DO IT ALL!

**What else can robots do? Check out some of their latest feats!**

TOPIO plays table tennis.

ROTi teaches English in elementary schools.

Moroman SDA10 flips pancakes.

Robonaut 2 helps astronauts aboard the International Space Station.

Watson plays *Jeopardy!*—and WINS!

→The researchers made up names for more than 1,000 toys and tested whether **Chaser** could identify them on command.

→ Chaser completed 838 of these tests over 3 years.

She never got fewer than 18 out of 20 correct.

**ultimate secret revealed!**

**Some dogs can understand the meanings of new words as quickly as toddlers.** How can canines have this ability? Experts say it all has to do with their origins. More than 15,000 years ago, humans tamed wolves to be the world's first domesticated animal—the dog. Humans and dogs began living side by side.

Like their wolf ancestors, dogs' brains are wired for obeying a pack leader. So most dogs are happy to listen to their human masters' commands. Over the years people have bred dogs for specific tasks like guarding, herding, and companionship. Dogs became naturally skilled at working closely with their owners, particularly picking up on voice commands and body language.

Today's dogs can be trained to do all kinds of tasks. They serve as guide dogs for people who can't see. They can help search for lost people after a disaster. Some dogs help police officers catch criminals.

## fact finder

# credits

**COVER**
(turtle), ChinaFotoPress/Getty Image; (jetpack), Courtesy of Martin Jetpack; (salamander), Jane Burton/naturepl.com; (robot), Marco Secchi/Getty Images for Paramount Home Entertainment; (dog), Ryan Cardone/Tidalstock; (cat), Tim Flach/Getty Images

**BACK COVER**
(gorillas), Eric Isselée/Shutterstock; (shark), Michael Patrick O'Neill/Alamy

2-3, Edgar Mueller/Getty Images; 4 (top), Jump Run Productions/Getty Images; 4 (bottom), Zhang Peng/Onasia .com; 5 (left), Dane Penland/Smithsonian Institution/Associated Press; 5 (right), Randy Olson/NationalGeographicStock.com

**CHAPTER 1: GOING TO EXTREMES**
6, Ryan Cardone; 8 (top), Jump Run Productions/Getty Images; 8 (bottom left), Andy Day/actionplus sports images/ Newscom; 8 (bottom right), Thomas Senf/Sportsandnews/ Sipa; 9, Gareth Lock; 9 (left center), Sergei Karpukhin/Reuters; 9 (right center), Jimmy Halliday/Getty Images; 9 (bottom), Harrison Shull/Aurora Photos/Corbis; 10-11, Mondolithic Studios Inc.; 12 (top), P. Psaïla/DoubleVue; 12 (bottom right), Denis Balibouse/Reuters; 12 (bottom left), courtesy of Crown Plaza, Copenhagen Towers; 13 (top), Lars Tunbjörk/ Agence Vu/Aurora Photos; 13 (left center), N55, Walking House, 2008. Commissioned by Wysing Arts Centre, England; 13 (right center), Tim Wimborne/Reuters; 13 (bottom), y60/ ZumaPress/Newscom; 14-15, Sindre Lundvold/Barcroft Meida/ Getty Images; 16 (top right), Creatas Images/Jupiterimages; 16 (top left), Photolibrary.com; 16 (bottom left), Detlev van Ravenswaay/Photo Researchers, Inc; 16 (bottom), Bryan and Cherry Alexander; 16 (bottom right), SuperStock; 17 (top), Frans Lanting/NationalGeographicStock.com; 17 (top left), Lawrence Lawry/PhotoDisc/PictureQuest; 17 (top right), NASA; 17 (bottom right), Todd White/NationalGeographicStock.com; 17 (bottom left), Shaffer–Smith/Getty Images; 18-19, Aguirre Emmanuel/Sipa/Newscom; 20 (top), Mark Clifford/Barcroft Media Ltd; 20 (bottom right), Karine Aigner/NG Staff; 20 (bottom left), Brian Cassey Photography; 21 (top right), Dean Pomerleau; 21 (top left), Peter Langone; 21 (bottom), Splash News/Newscom; 22-23, David B. Fleetham/SeaPics.com; 22, Alexander Hafemann/iStockphoto; 23, Fred Bavendam/ Minden/NationalGeographicStock.com; 24-25, Gregg Bleakney/ GBleakney.com

**CHAPTER 2: SEEING IS BELIEVING**
26, FLPA; 28 (top left), Karine Aigner/NG Staff; 28 (top right), Adam Gerrard/SWNS.com; 28 (bottom), Ross Parry Agency; 29 (bottom right), Murad Sezer/Associated Press; 29 (top), Adam Hartnett/Caters; 29 (top right), Courtesy of L. Sautner; 29 (bottom left), Jim Incledon; 30-31, Bence Mate/naturepl .com; 32 (bottom left), DLILLC/Corbis; 32 (top left), Tui De Roy/Minden Pictures; 32 (bottom center), Mark Payne–Gill/ naturepl.com; 32 (top center), Mark Payne–Gill/naturepl.com; 33 (bottom right), Constantinos Petrinos/naturepl.com; 33 (top right), Gary Bell/oceanwideimages.com; 33 (bottom left), Glaucomy Volans/naturepl.com; 33 (top left), Glaucomy Volans/ naturepl.com; 33 (bottom center), SuperStock; 33 (top center), SuperStock; 34 (top), ROX/rox.co.uk; 34 (right), Randy Olson/ NationalGeographicStock.com; 34 (bottom left), Joe Skipper/ Reuters; 35 (top), Issei Kato/Reuters; 35 (bottom left), Mike Clark/AFP/Getty Images; 35 (bottom right), WENN/Newscom; 36-37, YU Gallery, Paris, France; 38 (top right), Franck Fotos/ Alamy; 38 (top left), Franck Fotos/Alamy; 38 (bottom), Courtesy of Javier Senosiai; 39 (top), Franz Neumayr/Getty Images; 39 (center left), Johan De Meester/Ardea; 39 (center right), Julia Kuskin; 39 (bottom), Sean Gallup/Getty Images; 40 (left), Nick Garbutt/naturepl.com; 40 (right), Michael Nichols/ NationalGeographicStock.com; 41 (top), Ingram; 41 (center), Brandon Cole; 41 (bottom), Rob Friedman/iStockphoto.com; 42-43, Paul Macleod; 44 (right), Kevin Wick/Canstruction/0NC/ Newscom; 44 (left), Rex Features/Rex USA; 44 (bottom), Benoit Tessier/Reuters/Corbis; 45 (top), JTB Photo/ Photolibrary; 45 (bottom right), Zhang Peng/Onasia.com; 45 (bottom left), Invader/space–invaders.com

**CHAPTER 3: WHO'S COUNTING?**
46, Life on white/Alamy; 48 (top), Dorling Kindersley/Getty Images; 48 (bottom left), Chris Alleaume/National Geographic Your Shot; 48 (bottom right), Animals Animals/SuperStock; 49 (top left), Pete Oxford/Minden Pictures; 49 (top right), blickwinkel/Alamy; 49 (center), Werner Bollmann/Photolibrary .com; 49 (bottom), Cyril Ruoso/JH Editorial/Minden Pictures/ NationalGeographicStock.com; 50-51, David Fleetham/Getty Images; 51 (right), Eric Isselée/Shutterstock; 52-53, Yann Arthus–Bertrand/Altitude Henderson; 54-55, Hal Pierce/NASA's Goddard Space Flight Center; 54-55 (rhinos), Life on white/ Alamy; 56 (top), Richard Du Toit/Getty Images; 56 (center left), Masa Ushioda/SeaPics.com; 56 (center right), Bob Cranston/ SeaPics.com; 56 (bottom), Photodisc/Getty Images; 57 (top left), Jeremy Woodhouse/Photodisc Green/Getty Images; 57 (top right), Jean–Paul Ferrero/Minden Pictures; 57 (center), Tui De Roy/Minden Pictures; 57 (bottom left), imagebroker/ Alamy; 57 (bottom right), Superstock/Photolibrary.com; 58 (top left), Joel Sartore/NationalGeographicStock.com; 58 (top right), Tui De Roy/NationalGeographicStock.com; 58 (bottom), Wildlife GmbH/Alamy; 59 (left), Bangor University; 59 (right), Cisca Castelijns/Foto Natura/Minden Pictures/ NationalGeographicStock.com; 60-61 (giraffe), age fotostock/ SuperStock; 60-61 (ostriches), Four Oaks/Shutterstock; 60-61 (koalas), Life on white/Alamy; 60-61 (squirrel), Ingram; 62-63, Roy Gumpel/Touch Productions Ltd.; 64-65, Bill Draker/ Photolibrary.com; 64, Ingram

**CHAPTER 4: FREAKS OF NATURE**
66, Minden Pictures/SuperStock; 68, Yuji Sakai/Digital Vision/ Getty Images; 69 (top left), Milos Luzanin/Shutterstock; 69 (top right), saiko3p/Shutterstock; 69 (bottom left), Geoff Brightling/ Getty Images; 69 (bottom right), Jan Castricum/Minden Pictures; 70 (top), Paul Nicklen/NationalGeographicStock .com; 70 (left center), Winfried Wisniewski/Getty Images; 70 (right center), Konrad Wothe/Minden Pictures/ NationalGeographicStock.com; 70 (bottom), Frans Lanting Studio/Alamy; 71 (top left), Mike Anich/SuperStock; 71 (top right), Brandon Cole/Getty Images; 71 (center), Gerry Ellis/ Minden Pictures; 71 (bottom left), Buck Forester/Getty Images; 71 (bottom right), Suzi Eszterhas/Minden Pictures; 72-73, NASA; 74 (top), Biosphoto/Cèdric Girard; 74 (bottom left), Danita Delimont/Alamy; 74 (bottom right), Wesley A. Carr; 75 (top right), Ken Catania/Visuals Unlimited/Corbis; 75 (top left), Bruno Cavignaux/Biosphoto; 75 (bottom right), Ian Cruickshank/Alamy; 75 (bottom left), David A. Northcott/ Corbis; 76-77, Ultra_Generic/iStockphoto.com; 78 (left), Franco Tempesta; 78 (right), Maria Toutoudaki/Getty Images; 79 (top), Warren Photographic/Photo Researchers, Inc.; 79 (center), Digital Vision/Getty Images; 79 (frame), Ingram; 79 (bottom), F. G. Mayer/Photo Researchers, Inc.; 80-81, Petty Officer 2nd Class Lauren Jorgensen/U.S. Coast Guard/Associated Press; 82 (top), Spectrum Photofile/All Rights Reserved; 82 (center), Paul Hellstern/The Daily Oklahoman/Associated Press; 82 (bottom), Andrew G. Saffas; 83 (top left), Lyn Battle; 83 (top right), U.S. Navy, Official Photograph; 83 (bottom left), Spectrum Photofile/All Rights Reserved; 83 (bottom right), Jim Reed/Photo Researchers, Inc; 84 (bottom), Steve Hopkin/ Ardea.com; 84 (top left), Mike Hill/Getty Images; 84-85 (top right), Photodisc/Getty Images; 84-85 (Background), Dynamic Graphics/Creatas Images/Jupiter Images; 85 (left), Martha Holmes/NPL/Minden Pictures; 85, Tierfotoagentur/Alamy

**CHAPTER 5: ON THE MOVE**
86-87, Andy Rouse/naturepl.com; 88-89, Joffet Emmanuel/ Sipa; 90-91, STR News/Reuters; 92-93, Dr. Andreas Zeitler; 94 (top), Peter Mackay; 94 (center), David Kone/The American Visionary Art Museum; 94 (bottom), Harrod Blank; 95 (top left), Conference Bike by Eric Staller.com; 95 (top right), Harrod Blank; 95 (bottom left), Transtock/Corbis; 95 (bottom right), Inventist.com; 96-97, NGT; 96, Jean–Paul Ferrero/Auscape/ Minden Pictures; 97 (left), Joe McDonald/Woodfall/Photoshot; 97 (right), Beata Slonecka/NationalGeographicStock.com; 98 (top), Martin Ruegner/Getty Images; 98 (center left), Photolibrary.com; 98 (center right), Masa Ushioda/Alamy; 98 (bottom), Robert Kyllo/Shutterstock; 99 (top left), Juniors Bildarchiv/Alamy; 99 (top right), Punchstock; 99 (center), Michael Kevin Daly/Getty Images; 99 (bottom left), William Hadcliffe/Science Faction/Corbis; 99 (bottom right), A.T. Willett/ Alamy; 100-101, Nikada/iStockphoto.com; 102-103 (all), Harrod Blank; 104-105, Wayne Lynch/Corbis; 105 (top right), Amy Lane/Getty Images; 105 (top left), Marcus Jones/iStockphoto. com; 105 (bottom left), Henri Simon Faure/iStockphoto.com; 105 (bottom right), Ron Kimball/www.kimballstock.com

**CHAPTER 6: CLAIM TO FAME**
106, Adrian Dennis/Associated Press; 108 (top), Anthony Pidgeon/Lonely Planet; 108 (bottom left), c40/c40/ZUMA Press/Newscom; 108 (bottom right), Cui jian–Imaginechina/ Associated Press; 109 (top), Courtesy of Muvbox Concept; 109 (bottom), Courtesy of Events in the Sky; 110-111, Tyler Stableford/Getty Images; 112 (top), Courtesy of Teacups Puppies and Boutique; 112, (bottom) Courtesy of Las Ventanas al Paraiso, A Rosewood Resort; 113 (top right), Tim Flach/ Getty Images; 113 (top left), Melissa Pearcy; 113 (bottom right), Courtesy of La Petite Maison; 113 (bottom left), Candace Zynda; 114 (top), Corbis Premium RF/Alamy; 114 (bottom), gapper/Alamy; 115, Stephen Saks Photography/Alamy; 116-117, Clayton Hanmer; 118 (top), Stevie Mann; 118 (bottom), CB2/ZOB/Newscom; 119 (top), CB2/ZOB/WENN.com/ Newscom; 119 (center left), Kurt Vinion/Getty Images; 119 (center right), Kim Kyung–Hoon/Reuters/Corbis; 119 (bottom), Mr. Vincent Costello; 120, Kathy Willens/Associated Press; 120-121 (Background), Visions of America/SuperStock; 121 (top left), Associated Press; 121 (top right), Gary Sussman/ Associated Press; 121 (bottom left), Kevork Djansezian/ Associated Press; 121 (bottom right), Rob Carr/Associated Press; 122, Dane Penland/Smithsonian Institution/Associated Press; 123 (top left), Kristy Wigglesworth/Associated Press; 123 (top right), The Natural History Museum, London; 123 (bottom), ClassicStock/Alamy; 124 (top), Ancient Art & Architecture Collection Ltd/Alamy; 124 (bottom), Yiannis Papadimitriou/ Alamy; 125 (left), Paul Helm/Alamy; 125 (right), Michael Kappeler/Associated Press

**CHAPTER 7: WHAT ON EARTH?**
126, Jane Burton/naturepl.com; 128, ChinaFotoPress/Getty Images; 130-131, Bat Conservation; 132 (top), Darlyne A. Murawski/NationalGeographicStock.com; 132 (bottom left), courtesy of the Monterey Bay Aquarium Research Institute (c) 2004 MBARI; 132 (bottom right), Bruno Guenard/Photolibrary; 133 (top), Alexander Mustard; 133 (left center), Fred Bavendam/Minden Pictures; 133 (right center), David Shen/ Seapics.com; 133 (bottom), cs9/ZUMA Press/Newscom; 134-135, Ben Nottidge/Alamy; 135 (top), Phil Degginger/Alamy; 135 (bottom), Jason Edwards/NationalGeographicStock .com; 136 (left), Scott E. Barbour/Getty Images; 136 (right), Glow Images/SuperStock; 137 (top), Jon Warburton Lee; 137 (center left), Yoshio Tomii Photo Studio/Photolibrary.com; 137 (center right), James P. Blair/NationalGeographicStock.com; 137 (bottom), O. Luis Mazzatanta/NationalGeographicStock. com; 138-139, Carsten Peter/Speleo Research & Films/ NationalGeographicStock.com; 140-141, Design Pics/ SuperStock; 142, Photolibrary.com; 144 (left center), Armin Floreth/SuperStock; 144 (top), Franco Tempesta; 144 (bottom), Mark Horn/Getty Images; 144 (right center), DLILLC/Corbis; 145 (left center), AlaskaStock/Corbis; 145 (top), Christian Heinrich/SuperStock; 145 (bottom), SuperStock; 145 (right center), Doug Perrine/SeaPics.com

**CHAPTER 8: WILD & WACKY**
146-147, Buddy Mays/Corbis; 148 (top left), Zuma Press/ Newscom; 148 (top right), Rex USA; 148 (bottom), Quirky China News/Rex/Rex USA; 149 (top right), AFP/Getty Images; 149 (top left), Nadia Caffesse/Fulltiltphotography.com; 149 (bottom), Karen Portaleo/Highland Bakery; 149 (center), Liz Hickok; 150, Sean Wandzilak/iStockphoto.com; 151 (top), AptTone/Shutterstock; 151 (bottom), andersphoto/Shutterstock; 152-153, Mondolithic Studios Inc.; 154 (top), Shen Hong/ ZUMA Press; 154 (bottom right), Lionel Cironneu/Asssociated Press; 154 (bottom left), Mike Simons/Getty Images; 155 (top left), Mario Tama/Getty Images; 155 (bottom), Alberto Saiz/Associated Press; 155 (top right), Natthawat Wongrat/ ZUMA Press; 156, Steven J. Backman; 157 (top), Charles Whitehouse/*Yuma Daily Sun*/Associated Press; 157 (bottom), Stock Connection/SuperStock; 158, ZUMA Press/Corbis; 160 (top, both), Polaris; 160 (bottom left), Joao Sabino/Solent News/Rex/Rex USA; 160 (bottom right), Maria C. Valentino/ MCV Photo; 161 (top left), Rex/Rex USA; 161 (top right), Quirky China News/Rex/Rex USA; 161 (bottom right), Casey Gutteridge, CPG Photography; 161 (bottom left), Kobi Levi/ Solent News/Rex/Rex USA; 162-163, Barry Bland/Barcroft Media LTD; 164 (top left), PhotriMicroStock/L. Howe; 164 (top right), Buddy Mays/Corbis; 164 (bottom left), James P. Rowan; 164-165, Richard Cummins; 165 (top), Natalia Bratslavsky/ Alamy; 165 (center left), Dave and Sigrun Tollerton/Alamy; 165 (center right), David Barnes/Danita Delimont

**CHAPTER 9: INTELLIGENT LIFE**
166, Marco Secchi/Getty Images for Paramount Home Entertainment; 168 (top), Peter Charlesworth/OnAsia; 168-169, Chris Alleaume/National Geographic Your Shot; 169 (top left), Stuart Westmorland/DanitaDelimont.com; 169 (top right), Daniel Sambraus/Getty Images; 169 (center right), C. Dani/I. Jeske/De Agostini Picture Library/Getty Images; 169 (bottom), iStockphoto.com; 170-171, Mondolithic Studios Inc.; 172 (top), Courtesy of Martin Jetpack; 172 (bottom), NeuroSky, Inc. All Rights Reserved; 172-173, Kevin Hand; 173 (top), Brand X Pictures/Jupiter Images; 173 (bottom right), Courtesy of University of Washington; 173 (bottom left), Courtesy of Jonathan Black, Raytheon Company; 174-175, Stephan Morrell/NationalGeographicStock.com; 176-177 (all), Tom Nick Cocotos; 178-179, Image/Zuma Press; 180 (top left), David Cheskin–pa/Associated Press; 180 (top right), Jeffrey Sauger/WPN; 180 (bottom), Mason News Service; 181 (top), Paul Nicklen/National Geographic Stock; 181 (left), Corbis Premium RF/Alamy; 181 (right), Ron Kimball/Kimball Stock; 182-183, Randy Olson/NationalGeographicStock.com; 184, Mark Olencki/Wofford College; 185 (top left), Design Pics/ SuperStock; 185 (top right), fStop/SuperStock; 185, fStop/ SuperStock

## PUBLISHED BY THE NATIONAL GEOGRAPHIC SOCIETY

John M. Fahey, Jr., *Chairman of the Board and Chief Executive Officer*
Timothy T. Kelly, *President*
Declan Moore, *Executive Vice President; President, Publishing*
Melina Gerosa Bellows, *Executive Vice President; Chief Creative Officer, Books, Kids, and Family*

## PREPARED BY THE BOOK DIVISION

Nancy Laties Feresten, *Senior Vice President, Editor in Chief, Children's Books*; Jonathan Halling, *Design Director, Books and Children's Publishing*; Jay Sumner, *Director of Photography, Children's Publishing*; Jennifer Emmett, *Editorial Director, Children's Books*; Carl Mehler, *Director of Maps*; R. Gary Colbert, *Production Director*; Jennifer A. Thornton, *Managing Editor*

## STAFF FOR THIS BOOK

Robin Terry, *Project Editor*; Jennifer Emmett, Mary Varilla Jones, *Additional Editors*; James Hiscott, Jr., *Art Director*; Lori Epstein, Kelley Miller, Jay Sumner, *Illustrations Editors*; James Hiscott, Jr., Dawn McFadin, Rachael Hamm Plett, *Designers*; Julie Beer, Michelle Harris, *Researchers*; Kate Olesin, *Editorial Assistant*; Kathryn Robbins, *Design Production Assistant*; Hillary Moloney, *Illustrations Assistant*; Elizabeth Carney, Sarah Wassner Flynn, Ruth Musgrave, *Contributing Writers*; Grace Hill, *Associate Managing Editor*; Lewis R. Bassford, *Production Manager*; Susan Borke, *Legal and Business Affairs*

## MANUFACTURING AND QUALITY MANAGEMENT

Christopher A. Liedel, *Chief Financial Officer*; Phillip L. Schlosser, *Senior Vice President*; Chris Brown, *Technical Director*; Rachel Faulise, Nicole Elliott, and Robert L. Barr, *Managers*

Library of Congress Cataloging-in-Publication Data

Ultimate weird but true.
    p. cm. -- (Weird but true)
Includes index.
 ISBN 978-1-4263-0864-2 (hardcover : alk. paper) --
ISBN 978-1-4263-0895-6 (library binding : alk. paper)
 1. Curiosities and wonders--Juvenile literature.
 AG243.U45 2011
 031.02--dc23
                    2011020506

Scholastic ISBN: 978-1-4263-0978-6

Printed in U.S.A.
12/LPH-RRDW/3

## ACKNOWLEDGMENTS

*National Geographic Kids* gratefully acknowledges Karine Aigner, Madeline Franklin, Marilyn Terrell, Jeffrey Wandel, and Erin Whitmer for their contributions to *Ultimate Weird But True*. We would also like to thank the many scientists and experts who helped ensure that our facts are not only weird, but also true. While there are far too many to mention by name, the following people truly went the extra mile:

Jerry Bonnell, NASA's Goddard Space Flight Center; Richard Carlson, Carnegie Institution for Science; Dennis Desjardin, Department of Biology, San Francisco State University; Michael E. Dillon, Department of Zoology and Physiology, University of Wyoming; Paolo Forti, Italian Institute of Speleology, University of Bologna; Sharon Gursky-Doyen, Department of Anthropology, Texas A & M University; Andrea Heydlauff, Panthera; Lauren Jorgensen, 9th District Public Affairs, United States Coast Guard; Dave Mellinger, NOAA/PMEL VENTS Program, Hatfield Marine Science Center, Oregon State University; Chris Orban, Brown University; Michael Reeder, School of Mathematical Sciences, Monash University; Frank M. Rinderknecht, Rinspeed, Inc.; Rosa Rugani, Department of Psychology, University of Padova; Bill Sanders, Museum of Paleontology, University of Michigan; J. G. M. "Hans" Thewissen, Department of Anatomy and Neurobiology, Northeastern Ohio Universities Colleges of Medicine and Pharmacy; Chih-Shiue Yan, Geophysical Laboratory, Carnegie Institution of Washington.

National Geographic's net proceeds support vital exploration, conservation, research, and education programs.

For more information, please call 1-800-NGS LINE (647-5463) or write to the following address:
National Geographic Society
1145 17th Street N.W.
Washington, D.C. 20036-4688 U.S.A.

Visit us online at nationalgeographic.com/books
For librarians and teachers: ngchildrensbooks.org
More for kids from National Geographic:
kids.nationalgeographic.com

For information about special discounts for bulk purchases, please contact National Geographic Books Special Sales: ngspecsales@ngs.org

For rights or permissions inquiries, please contact National Geographic Books Subsidiary Rights: ngbookrights@ngs.org

## ANATOMY OF A WEIRD-BUT-TRUE FACT

How does a fact make it into a Weird But True book?

First, it has to be WEIRD. Our team of editors and writers scour the news, the latest discoveries, Internet gems, urban legends, wacky myths, and tantalizing tidbits to find a fact that's really weird.

It also has to be TRUE. So our researchers check every single word to make sure the fact is 100% accurate.

It has to LOOK COOL. Our photo editors and designers find the perfect weird picture or the most dazzling weird design to make each fact jump out at you.

It has to BE FUN by itself and also as a book. So we put it all together in an amazing-looking book that's so much fun you can't put it down.

Here's a weird-but-true fact about *Ultimate Weird But True*: It took an ultimate team of 5 editors, 3 writers, 4 designers, 4 photo editors, 2 researchers, more than 20 experts, and at least 10 others to make it the weirdest, truest, most ultimate book around.